Regional and Local Powers in Europe

Education and Youth, Culture, Public Health, Transeuropean Networks and Regional and Structural Policy

CoR Studies E-4/2002

Brussels, April 2002

This study was produced by external experts under the direction of the Europäisches Zentrum für Föderalismus-Forschung, University of Tübingen, Germany. It does not represent the official views of the Committee of the Regions.

A great deal of additional information on the European Union is available on the Internet.
It can be accessed through the Europa server (http://europa.eu.int).

Cataloguing data can be found at the end of this publication.

Luxembourg: Office for Official Publications of the European Communities, 2002

ISBN 92-895-0151-0

© European Communities, 2002
Reproduction is authorised provided the source is acknowledged.

Printed in Belgium

PRINTED ON WHITE CHLORINE-FREE PAPER

EUROPEAN UNION

Committee of the Regions

Preface

One of the greatest challenges facing the European Union today is how to increase its legitimacy in the eyes of European citizens. It must begin by ensuring that citizens know who does what in Europe. Likewise, if people are to rally to the major objectives of the Union, they will want the European Union to be more in touch, and to pay more attention to their specific concerns. In preparation for a new Intergovernmental Conference, scheduled for 2004, the Laeken European Council therefore took the initiative of convening a Convention composed of the main parties involved in the debate on the future of the Union.

The priorities of the Convention, which has the task of considering the key issues raised by the European Union's future development, include a better distribution and definition of competence between the Union and the Member States, and greater democratic legitimacy and transparency in existing institutions.

By giving the Committee of the Regions a political and institutional role, the Treaty on European Union placed the representatives of the towns and regions of Europe at the heart of the decision-making process. Its main task is to help ensure respect for the principles governing the distribution of responsibilities and competence between the Union, State and the local and regional authorities, which are the decision-making levels closest to European citizens.

Against this background, this study gives an overview of the powers of local and regional authorities in the Union in areas in which the Committee of the Regions has for the first time been given a consultative role, i.e. education and youth, culture, public health, trans-European networks and regional policy. It emphasises the diversity of local and regional bodies in the European Union, and national or regional differences in the implementation of these policies.

Through its observers at the Convention, the Committee of the Regions will seek to capitalise on this remit so as to ensure that the powers of local and regional authorities are more in keeping with their growing responsibilities.

A. Bore
President of the Committee of the Regions

Table of Contents

I.	Introduction	1
II.	Sharing Responsibilities – The Territorial Structures of the EU Member States	17
	1. *Systems of Shared Responsibility*	17
	2. *Country Profiles of Federal EU Member States*	21
	2.1 Austria	21
	2.2 Belgium	22
	2.3 Germany	24
	3. *Country Profiles of Regionalised EU Member States*	26
	3.1 France	26
	3.2 Italy	28
	3.3 Portugal	30
	3.4 Spain	32
	3.5 United Kingdom	34
	4. *Country Profiles of Decentralised EU Member States*	37
	4.1 Denmark	37
	4.2 Finland	39
	4.3 The Netherlands	40
	4.4 Sweden	41
	5. *Country Profiles of Two-Tiered EU Member States*	43
	5.1 Greece	43
	5.2 Ireland	45
	5.3 Luxembourg	47

III.	**Joint Policy-Making in the Maastricht Fields of Mandatory Consultation: Forms of Cooperation and Coordination**	**49**
	1. *Systems of Joint-Policy Making and Multi-Level Governance*	*49*
	2. *Federal States*	*52*
	2.1 Austria	52
	2.2 Belgium	54
	2.3 Germany	56
	3. *Regionalised States*	*57*
	3.1 France	57
	3.2 Italy	58
	3.3 Portugal	60
	3.4 Spain	62
	3.5 United Kingdom	63
	4. *Decentralised States*	*65*
	4.1 Denmark	65
	4.2 Finland	66
	4.3 The Netherlands	68
	4.4 Sweden	70
	5. *Two-Tiered States*	*71*
	5.1 Greece	71
	5.2 Ireland	73
	5.3 Luxembourg	75

IV.	National Surveys on the Distribution of Tasks within the "Maastricht Fields" of Mandatory CoR Consultation	77

	1.	*General Training and Youth*	*77*
		1.1 Federal States	83
		1.2 Regionalised States	89
		1.3 Decentralised States	100
		1.4 Two-Tiered States	109
	2.	*Culture*	*115*
		2.1 Federal States	123
		2.2 Regionalised States	127
		2.3 Decentralised States	133
		2.4 Two-Tiered States	137
	3.	*Public Health*	*141*
		3.1 Federal States	147
		3.2 Regionalised States	150
		3.3 Decentralised States	157
		3.4 Two-Tiered States	161
	4.	*Transeuropean Networks*	*165*
		4.1 Federal States	171
		4.2 Regionalised States	175
		4.3 Decentralised States	183
		4.4 Two-Tiered States	187
	5.	*Regional and Structural Policy*	*191*
		5.1 Federal States	201
		5.2 Regionalised States	211
		5.3 Decentralised States	227
		5.4 Two-Tiered States	139

V. Conclusions for the Future Work of the Committee of the Regions   249

VI. Bibliography   261

I. Introduction

The present report forms part of an overall research project commissioned by the Committee of the Regions (CoR) which shall evaluate the local and regional powers in all fields of CoR mandatory consultation according to the Treaty establishing the European Community (TEC). In a first step, an international research team composed of Professor Dr. Rudolf Hrbek, University of Tuebingen, Germany, Professor Dr. Frank Delmartino, University of Leuven, Belgium, and Professor Dr. Dr. Jörg Monar, University of Leicester, United Kingdom, and coordinated by the European Centre for Research on Federalism, University of Tuebingen, was asked to elaborate a study on the "Regional and Local Powers in Europe" dealing with the five policy areas Social Policy, Employment, Vocational Training, Environment and Transport. The remaining policy fields where the TEC has already provided for mandatory CoR consultation since Maastricht, namely General Training and Youth, Culture, Public Health, Guidelines and Actions for the Construction of Trans-European Networks (TEN), and, last but not least, European Regional and Structural Policy (including the European Social Fund, the European Regional Development Fund and the Cohesion Fund) have been analysed in an additional research project and are presented in this second study[1].

---

[1] The European Centre for Research on Federalism (ECRF) takes complete responsibility for the text of the study. Any mistakes, incorrect or imprecise formulation fall under the exclusive responsibility of the ECRF. However, it should be considered that the territorial structures of the EU Member States are subject to a political decision and are adapted from time to time. The current study reflects the status of the territorial structure in the Member States of May 2001.

Comparing the research agenda for this second study with the first project, certain adaptations have been made in light of the experience of the first project. The approach taken by the research team includes the analysis of the following aspects:

- An introductory overview on the territorial structure in the 15 EU Member States (chapter II);

- An analysis of formalised and informal ways of cooperation, including political channels of access and an assessment of the influence of subnational players in political practice within the five policy fields examined (chapter III);

- A comparative description of the formal distribution of legislative and/or executive tasks between the national, regional and local level in the 15 EU Member States for each of the five fields of mandatory CoR consultation since Maastricht;

- Finally, the research team was asked to give recommendations as concerns strategic priorities for the future activities of the CoR within the five policy areas in order to consolidate its role as "focal point" of regional and local cooperation at supranational level.

The research team has been asked to present the findings in tabular form for each policy field and Member State. The tabular form provides a short, but nevertheless comprehensive overview on the distribution of tasks in the 15 Member States. As a tabular overview, cannot fully reflect the complex interaction between different levels of government, which is a typical feature of policy making especially in federal states; the tabular overviews should be read as complement to the chapter on the cooperation and coordination between the different levels (Chapter III). In this chapter, both general forms of cooperation and specific characteristics of the five policy fields are described and analysed. It has already been mentioned in the introduction to the first study that the policy making in the EU Member States is characterised by a joint-policy-making and specific forms of multi-level governance in a large number of policy fields. With respect to the policy fields examined in this second study, this characteristic is especially true for the policy field of Regional and Structural Policy. The policy field of Regional and Structural Policy also demonstrates very clearly the interrelation and interdependence of activities at the EU, the national and sub-national levels, national policies and sub-national activities. These patterns of interdependence and interrelation of different tiers of government can properly only be presented in a better way in text form.

The five policy fields of General Training and Youth, Culture, Public Health, TEN and Regional and Structural Policy are to a certain degree interrelated with each other and with other EU– and national policies. This intersection of policy fields shall be demonstrated already in this introduction by giving some examples:

- A close link can be identified in many Member States between General Training Policy and Vocational Training, as both policy fields are designed to provide young people skills needed for professional life. Following the principle of life-long learning, there is no clear dividing line between the learning for professional life and general training.

- A further example of the overlap of policy fields is the area of Transeuropean Networks and Regional and Structural Policy, with certain activities in the area of Transeuropean Networks being additionally financed by the European Regional Fund or Cohesion Fund, with the projects of TEN having an important impact on the regional development of the country / region.

- For Culture, a significant interdependence with other policy fields can be observed in the national systems of the Member States. In many EU Member States (as for example Belgium and Germany) General Training and Culture are closely interrelated. General Training is characterised in many Member States as belonging to "cultural affairs". Sub-national players have an important function in this policy field, especially in federal states.

Turning from the interrelation and intersection of the five policy fields examined in this study to the scope and orientation of the policy fields, it has to be emphasised that, taken as a general characteristic, scope and understanding of the policy fields in the national context are much broader and include more areas than the respective EU policy. Typical examples are again Culture and General Training and Youth, with Culture in the Member States focussing also and more pronounced on cultural activities and institutions at regional and local level. General Training Policy is also much broader in the national context of the Member States, as it includes curricula of school and post-school education and the setting up of a structured educational system, which educates young people according to their needs and capacities.

Furthermore some general considerations on the model of governance, which had already been analysed in the research project on the "Regional and Local Powers in Europe: Employment Policy, Social Policy, Environment, Transport and Vocational Training" need to be recalled, as they can be observed for the "Maastricht Fields of Mandatory Consultation" as well. Within the current discussion on the form of governance in the EU related to the White Paper published by the Commission, these aspects of governance are of central importance for the future development of the EU. As already described in the first report, the tendency of joint decision-making beyond clearly defined policy fields and across different levels as an expression of the political reality of multi-level governance in the European Union has strongly been favoured by the new policy-making approach of the European Commission: "In general, the emergence of complex problems highlights the limits of the Commission's policy-making and executive abilities and...it is significant that it has recently begun to stress the need to seek ways of *coordinating* the resources and abilities of players at lower levels both for the generation of information and for the implementation of policies in a context where it has found that its existing tools under the Treaty are inadequate. The Better Lawmaking initiative of recent years focusing on how the Commission is implementing the principles of subsidiarity and proportionality also testifies to a certain transformation in the forms of governance at the European level and to the need to develop and diffuse them more widely. This initiative seeks to achieve the benefits offered by such methods as consultation by Green papers, which aim to inform the legislative process more adequately, and Framework Directives, where means of implementation are left for lower level decisions." (Lebessis/Paterson 1997, p. 11). It is not at least due to this move from rigid and top-down regulation to a flexible and inclusive process of collective learning if the Commission applies new instruments, which leave more leeway for national, regional or local action in the implementation in various programmes and measures. A typical case is the implementation of the EU General Training and Youth programmes in the Member States as well as on the regional and local level. For these evolving patterns of European "multi-level" or "polycentric" governance, some observers conclude that "it becomes difficult, indeed almost impossible, to reason in terms of competence levels" (Le Galès 1998, p. 244). However, this conclusion seems little differentiated. In order to assess adequately the significance of the distribution of responsibilities within the Member States, one has to shift the emphasis from the overall view of "multi-level governance" to the bottom-up view of the "policy capacity" of sub-national governments. This different perspective may be expressed as follows: "In the past, the key question to ask about territorial governments was to do with their degree of autonomy, that is the ability to do things without interference from higher levels. In an interdependent world, autonomy in this sense is less important. More important is policy capacity - that is the ability to act on public issues to change outcomes. Policy capacity depends on the regional government's powers and resources and its ability to link sectoral networks in space." (Keating 1998, p. 135) With the explicit reference to the powers and resources of regional and – as has to be added – local entities, this point of view brings more clearly to the fore that the allocation of tasks between different levels of governments in the political systems of the Member States has not become obsolete despite of the interlocking patterns of decision-making that are symptomatic for polycentric governance in the European Union. Indeed, the European Commission has recently started to rethink the patterns of EU policy-making in a way that seems to be closely related to this very concept of "policy capacity". In the communication "Shaping the New

Europe" dealing with the strategic objectives of its working programme for the period 2000-2005, the Commission has announced the intention to publish a White Paper on "New Forms of European Governance" by summer 2001 (European Commission 2000a, p. 7). Starting from the observation that there is nowadays "hardly any sector of social and economic activity not affected by European Union policy and legislation, and where authorities in the Member States are not part and parcel of European governance" (European Commission 2000a, p. 6), the Commission stresses the need for a new, more democratic division of labour between the Commission, the other European institutions, the Member States, their sub-national authorities and civil society which overcomes the publicly perceived remoteness of "Brussels" and allows for greater transparency, accountability and a more participatory, "hands-on" democracy in Europe. As the President of the European Commission, Romano Prodi, has stressed in its presentation of the working programme to the European Parliament, one of the main problems in this context is that there has been no overall "master plan" under which European policies were designed and coordinated until now (Prodi 2000, p. 4).

According to the Commission's plan, the preparation of the White Paper on "New Forms of European Governance" has to be guided by two basic premises in order to improve the consistency between Community policies and to guarantee democratically legitimate EU institutions that operate effectively in a transparent and accountable way enjoying the full confidence of the citizens. On the one hand, the Commission pleads for the creation of new forms of partnership between the different levels of government in Europe. President Prodi has stressed in this context that "we have to stop thinking in terms of hierarchical layers of competence separated by the subsidiarity principle and start thinking, instead, of a networking arrangement, with all levels of governance shaping, proposing, implementing and monitoring policy together" (Prodi 2000, p. 5). On the other hand, however, this cross-level approach towards a "Network Europe" is far from denying the need for a more clear-cut delimitation of powers in the multi-level system of the EU since the concept highlights at once that the time has come for more delegation and decentralisation of tasks with the European Commission refocussing on core activities and that future forms of EU governance will have to pay greater attention to the principle of subsidiarity, the principle related to the question "what should be done at European level and what should be done by the Member States, the Regions or civil society" (Prodi 2000, p. 5). Presenting the new strategic objectives to the Committee of the Regions, the President of the European Commission has explicitly acknowledged that particularly the importance of regional authorities will considerably increase in the coming years due to the fact that "many national States are adopting federal forms of government, and important areas for action in the European domain are being opened up for regional institutions" and due to the opening up of a "major public debate how to move on from the decentralisation of administrative competences to a genuine autonomy of government at regional level" (Prodi, 2000a, p. 2). Obviously, the regional and local bodies in the European Union must not disregard that the first statements of the Commission which deal with its new concept of "European governance" have not gone beyond the concrete announcement to decentralise "day-to-day executive" responsibilities, so far (European Commission 2000a, p. 7). And it is not at least for that reason that the Committee of the Regions – also representing sub-national bodies vested with legislative powers – should pay special attention to being actively involved in the policy related to the White Paper.

On 25 July 2001, the European Commission presented the White Paper on Governance. In its communication, the Commission emphasises that the White Paper proposes far-reaching changes to the way the Union develops and implements its policies. Five principles have been identified as cornerstones for the future development of the EU policies. These principles are openness, participation, accountability, effectiveness and coherence. These principles shall guide the Union in its policy making and institutional development. The principles shall contribute to the achievement of the underlying objective of bringing the Union closer to the citizens. The White Paper can be structured into three main sections, which provide for key proposals on governance, institutional aspects to implement the reform of European governance and the definition and distribution of powers, political responsibilities and competencies on the one hand between the EU institutions and on the other hand between the EU, its Member States and regions.

In a first step, dealing with general proposals for the future governance of the EU, the Commission's White Paper proposes to structure the relationship with civil society. For this purpose, a code of conduct for the consultation of organisations representing the European civil society shall be established, which identifies the responsibilities and improves the accountability of all partners. This measure shall contribute to an improved relationship between EU and civil society structures. Secondly, and probably most importantly for the CoR, the Commission proposes to make greater use of the skills and practical experience of regional and local players. Even though the integration of regional and local authorities in the European policy-making process is primarily an issue of the national authorities and follows the national rules and procedures, the European Commission committed itself to a more systematic dialogue with the associations of regions and cities already at an early stage of the policy process. Thirdly, the EU shall build confidence in the way policy makers use expert advice. In order to achieve this general objective, the Commission will develop guidelines to open up the system for the use of experts to greater public scrutiny and debate. Fourthly, the policy objectives shall be defined more clearly. The effectiveness of policy-making shall be improved by combining legislation with non-legislative and self-regulatory solutions. These reforms shall contribute to simplifying and speeding up the legislative process. As fifth element of the general reform of EU governance, the conditions for establishing EU regulatory agencies shall be defined. According to the Commission's White Paper, these agencies can reinforce the effectiveness of EU law in the eyes of both business and public by bringing decisions in some of the most complex and technical areas closer to the people affected. Finally, the roles and responsibilities of each EU Institution shall be refocused. By this shaping of the institutional balance, the citizens shall be enabled to hold political leaders and their institutions responsible for the decisions taken on the EU level.

The institutional reform and the reshaping of the institutional design, which shall focus on the Commission, Council and European Parliament, form an essential, integral part of the shaping of European governance. In this respect, the Commission shall make a more targeted use of its right of initiative. Furthermore, the consultations and involvement of expert advise and impact assessment shall be improved. By these means, a more critical and selective consideration of the need for political initiatives shall be achieved. Secondly, the EU legislation shall be reduced to the essential and concentrate on setting out a framework on the form of implementation. The

Council and European Parliament should focus on political direction and content, while leaving the implementation to the executive. Finally, the national and regional players shall be involved more effectively in the shaping, application and enforcement of Community rules and programmes. These forms of involvement will result from the proposals of dialogue, decentralisation, improved cooperation and a more effective enforcement of Community law.

Additionally, the White Paper deals with the distribution of competencies and political responsibility between the institutions as well as between the EU and its Member States. With respect to the first dimension, the distribution of competencies between the legislature and executive, the model should follow that of national democracies. Where decisions are taken jointly be the Council and the European Parliament, those two institutions should enjoy equal roles in monitoring execution. Furthermore and at the same time, this clarification of roles must allow the Commission to assume full executive responsibility. Additionally, the Union needs clear principles identifying how competence is shared between the Union and its Member States. For that purpose, a common concept has to be found to regulate, which issues shall be dealt with on European level and which topics shall be left to the Member States and regions.

The Commission aims at establishing a consultative process, starting immediately after the publication of the White Paper and which will last until the end of March 2002. By that time, the Commission will report on the progress made and the further development of the White Paper.

By giving a first assessment to the proposals in the White Paper, it seems of major importance for the regions within the EU and the CoR that the Commission formally acknowledges the important role of the regions in the shaping and re-shaping of European governance. Within major EU policies, especially with respect the Regional and Structural Policy, the regions form the essential link between the EU and the civil society, between the EU decision-making system and the public being affected by it. A comprehensive analysis of the White Paper, of European governance and of its impact for the regional and local level in Europe would be beyond the scope and purpose of the present study. However, three dimensions related to the topic of the EU White Paper shall be discussed:

- the form of cooperation between the European Commission, European institutions and the regions;
- the impact of the new forms of governance envisaged by the European Commission on the field of mandatory consultation examined in the present study;
- the consequences of the new approach to governance for the Committee of the Regions.

The European Commission attributes a high political value to the cooperation between the European institutions and the national, regional and local authorities. The White Paper expresses the explicit aim to increase the cooperation and to use the knowledge and experience of the regional and local authorities. In the White Paper, the Commission emphasises explicitly the concept of openness and cooperation with Member States, regions and local authorities. Even though the Commission welcomes the participation of the regions in the communication process, it attributes the tasks of the institutionalisation of cooperation with the local authorities explicitly to the Member States. Within the approach for the cooperation favoured by the European Commission, the form of cooperation should be concentrated on the regions and their associations. The White Paper does not make explicit reference to the CoR with respect to the approach of increased cooperation. In this respect, the CoR should consider to raise its profile as representation of regional and local interests, as source of information for the community legislation process and for the other European institutions. As the Commission explicitly recognises that the EU policies have an increasing impact on the regional and local level, the CoR might be able to establish itself as a significant player in the emerging network of coordination and consultation. In its concept of governance, the European Commission implements a network approach for the restructuring of the cooperation and policy coordination. The European Commission aims at establishing a network as new form of governance and interrelation of different tiers of government. The improved involvement of various networks, grassroots organisations as well as national, regional and local authorities shall lead, according to the Commission's White Paper, to a multi-level partnership. Within this partnership, the national governments shall involve their regions and cities in the European policy-making and shall foresee adequate consultation mechanisms. In addition to the European and national associations of regions, the civil society and expert advices shall be effectively integrated in the policy-making. By making use of these various sources of information, the European Commission aims at establishing flexible and thematically orientated networks, which contribute to an effective and efficient law-making process. The Commission aims at rationalising and structuring the consultation and dialog by establishing a code of conduct for these forms of cooperation. The CoR should establish itself as source of information and significant player in the current restructuring process.

The second aspect to be analysed is the impact of the new approach to governance on the field of mandatory consultation. In this respect it is important to emphasise that the Commission's White Paper makes only comparatively limited explicit reference to certain policy fields. However, with the general concept of the White Paper focussing on the participation of various players and the network approach, certain consequences for the policy field of mandatory consultation can be identified. The concept of participation and the cooperation is of specific importance with respect to Regional and Structural Policy. In this policy field, the regional and local authorities are very active and are closely integrated in the policy making process in most EU Member States. Therefore, they have a high level of experience and knowledge in this policy field, which can and should be used by the European institutions. Furthermore, two specific proposals for new forms of governance have significant influence on the field of mandatory consultation of the CoR. Firstly, the European Commission proposes to use better and faster regulations and a more flexible approach to policy tools. According to the Commission's proposals, only the basic framework is to be regulated by community legislation, whereas the bulk is to be governed by regulatory agencies or executive bodies. The shift in policy regulation would imply a shift from political institutions taking part in the legislative process to them being in charge of policy implementation and would reduce the CoR's scope for influencing policy-making. The shift requires that the CoR reorganises its approach. In addition to fulfilling its tasks in the legislative process, the CoR should also contribute with its experience and knowledge to the implementation process of those legislative acts, which might be assigned to future executive agencies. This applies both to community advisory committees and external bodies, as for example expert advice.

Finally and in summing up the assessment of the White Paper, some further implications for the CoR shall be mentioned. The European Commission mentions the Committee of the Regions explicitly in the context of the approach to a better involvement of regional and local players as well as of the civil society in the law making process. The White Paper considers the CoR as one of the complementing channels of influencing the policy making, which contributes the regional and local perspective to the legislative process. The CoR should take fully account of the various channels of access used by the Commission and should take account of opinions published by other institutions. In doing so, the CoR should focus on those tasks, which have a genuine regional or local dimension. It should focus on areas in which the CoR can provide added value by providing input in the legislative process. In this context and with respect to the transfer of policy-implementation tasks to executive agencies, a more pro-active approach to consultation, which provides advice at an early stage is an essential element of an effective participation in the new model of governance envisaged by the Commission.

In summing up the plans of the Commission for new forms of EU governance the expectation is justified that, in political reality, the relevance of the concept of "policy capacity" and the "network approach" will further increase the potential for regional and local entities to establish themselves as players in European policy-making. This approach will stress both the importance of the distribution of competencies between the different levels of government within the EU and the principles of partnership and cross-level governance in the multi-level system of the Union.

II. Shared Responsibilities – The Territorial Structures of the EU Member States

1. *Systems of Shared Responsibility*

The territorial organisation of the fifteen Member States of the European Union and the respective distribution of powers differ considerably with respect to the status and formal degree of autonomy of sub-national entities. Nevertheless, it is possible to regroup them into four general categories: countries with a federal structure (federal states), countries with a multi-level structure, subdivided into regionalised and decentralised states, and states with a two-level structure (two-tiered states) without an intermediate, i.e. regional, level. This classification was already used for the first project on the "Amsterdam Fields of Mandatory Consultation".

States with a multi-level structure show substantial differences concerning the legal basis of competencies devolved to sub-national entities, i.e. devolution may be constitutionally entrenched or go back to ordinary law. Especially within the sub-category of regionalised states, we often find asymmetric patterns of devolution in the sense that regions within one state are endowed with a different degree of autonomy, e.g. in Italy and Spain.

Table 1 summarises the basic features of the four different categories of EU Member States.

Table 1: Different Categories of EU Member States

1. Federal States	Regional authorities (elected) with genuine legislative powers, institutionalised participation in federal level decision-making; three-level systems
2. States with a multi-level structure	
a) Regionalised States	Regional authorities (elected) with restricted legislative powers, substantial autonomy, no or weakly institutionalised participation in federal level decision-making; three level systems
b) Decentralised States	Sub-ordinate intermediate authorities above the local level, qualified autonomy, no legislative powers
3. Two-tiered States	Two tiers of government comprising the national and local level, no regional level

In political reality there are particular difficulties to distinguish federal states clearly from regionalised states.

In classical *federal states* like Germany we find a very complex system of joint decision-making of different levels in formulating, implementing and funding of policies (the so-called "Politikverflechtung"), which has emerged over the years. While it is relatively easy to outline the distribution of competencies in the field of legislation (with a clear predominance of the national level in political practice), it is much more difficult to delimitate competencies concerning the actual implementation of legislation. In the political reality of most federal states we find strong tendencies towards "cooperative federalism" which is characterised by the existence of many different types of mixed councils, advisory boards and other institutions composed of representatives from the national and regional level established to coordinate the implementation of national law by sub-national authorities. Competencies often overlap between federal and regional institutions. In addition, there are regularly numerous mechanisms and institutions for the horizontal coordination of activities at the regional level. In federal systems the national and regional governments regularly act as partners, although specific rights are usually reserved to the exclusive competence of the national level. Within the European Union there are three federal states: Austria, Belgium and Germany.

In *regionalised states* some substantial competencies have been devolved from the national level – either to the regional level in general or to single regions with a special status. Nevertheless, the national level remains dominant. In most of the states belonging to this category, the regional tier is foreseen by the constitution, yet there are some cases where the constitution does not provide for this third level, i.e. the intermediate level between the national and the local level. This is, for example, the case in France where the "Régions" were introduced by the laws on decentralisation from 1982 and 1986, although the French constitution does not provide for the establishment of these sub-national bodies. Despite this lack of an explicit constitutional basis, this country must be qualified as "regionalised state" due to the extent of competencies devolved to the French regions and the strong democratic legitimacy of their directly elected assemblies[2]. Other Member States of the

---

[2] Certain authors disagree with this form of classification, as all three entities in France (Région, Département, Commune) are classified as "pouvoirs locaux" according to the

European Union belonging to this group of countries are Italy, Spain, the United Kingdom, and Portugal. For these regionalised states, it is typical that they provide for different degrees of legislative autonomy at the regional level. As concerns Italy with its 20 regions, there exist only five regions with a special statute. In Spain the 17 Autonomous Communities have different levels of responsibilities because of the differences in their statutes and the various transfer processes. Similar differences may be found in the United Kingdom after the asymmetric devolution of powers to Wales, Scotland and Northern Ireland, which recently took place. And finally, Portugal has endowed only the island groups of Madeira and the Azores with regional autonomy, while the territorial organisation of the mainland remains highly centralised.

In the *decentralised states* of the European Union, i.e. Denmark, Finland, the Netherlands and Sweden, regional authorities are not vested with real legislative autonomy vis-à-vis the central government. Regional authorities are often territorial departments of national ministries or boards, which are created for organisational reasons.

Only three states of the European Union still have a *two-level structure*: Ireland, Greece and Luxembourg. Ireland and Luxembourg are small states, where the creation of a third level has not been that important for organisational reasons. However, there are efforts to intensify interregional cooperation between Irish counties at the moment, which might change the former centralistic structure of Ireland. In Greece, a process of decentralisation

---

French constitution. However, in taking a political science perspective and for the above stated reasons, the classification of France as regionalised state is justified.

is going on which has included the formal transfer of some competencies to a third level.

Table 2: Classification of EU Member States

1. Federal States	Austria, Belgium, Germany
2. Regionalised States	France, Italy, Portugal, Spain, United Kingdom
3. Decentralised States	Denmark, Finland, Netherlands, Sweden
4. Two-tiered States	Greece, Ireland, Luxembourg

2. Country Profiles of Federal EU Member States

2.1 Austria

Austria is a federal state with three constitutionally defined levels of government: the federation (Bund), nine states (Länder) and the municipalities (Gemeinden). There is strong predominance of the federal government as concerns legislation whereas implementing tasks are largely with the Länder and the local level. The Austrian federal system is often characterized as rather weak because the most important fields of legislation are explicitly attributed to the federal level and the Länder exert only little influence on federal decision-making via the Austrian Bundesrat (parliamentary 2-chamber system). Exclusive Länder jurisdiction is restricted to very few fields and the financial administration is an exclusive federal responsibility. The most important areas of Länder legislative power are the status of local authorities *("Gemeinderecht")*, spatial planning, building law, town and country planning, environmental protection *("Naturschutz")*, tourism, culture and sports. This assessment largely neglects, however, that there exist several informal channels for the Länder to represent their interests at federal level. This holds especially true for the very strong Länder organisations of the political parties and the "Conference of Land Governors" *("Landeshauptmännerkonferenz")*. Furthermore, politics in Austria have been characterised by very close forms of concerted action between various social players in the policy-making process – social partners, political parties, and associations. Even though this general characterisation is still valid, the importance of the social partnership has decreased in recent years. This involves also the Länder, and therefore, the real influence of the Länder is more important than their formal competencies would suggest. As concerns the local level, the municipalities are endowed with the right of self-government.

Reforms of the federal system have been a frequently discussed topic in Austria and the Länder urged for far-reaching constitutional amendments in the run-up to EU membership to strengthen their autonomy. However, until now most of these efforts failed due to the disagreement on financial questions.

2.2 Belgium

Belgium has become a federal state through various state reforms beginning in 1970 and lasting with four successive state reforms until 1993. The process of state-reform is however an ongoing process that arrived at a new stage in 2001 by voting of a series of additional reforms by the Federal Parliament, based on the Lambermont agreement of 2000 that defined e.g.: a transfer of competences from the federal level to the regions and communities.

Since the reform of 1993, the federal principle is included in the constitution in article 1. Belgian federalism is a model *sui generis* which is hardly comparable to classical federal systems. This singularity can be traced back to five basic features. First of all, the federal state did not emerge from the unification of formerly sovereign entities but from the devolution of competencies from the originally centralised state to newly created sub-national bodies, i.e. the regions and communities. This *centrifugal impetus* of federalising the Belgian state has never come to a halt and many observers agree meanwhile that Belgium is more similar to a confederation than to a federation. This development is in stark contrast to centralising tendencies, which have characterised intergovernmental relations in federal states like Germany or Austria from the beginning. The second outstanding feature of the Belgian federal system is its *bipolar structure*. The successive state reforms in Belgium have resulted from ongoing conflicts between the two linguistic groups of the Dutch-speaking and French-speaking parts of the population. These conflicts have a linguistic, economic and ideological dimension. Furthermore, Belgium constitutes with regard to the intermediate levels of government a *dual federation* with the three "communities" (the Flemish, French and German-speaking Community), on the one hand, responsible for legislative matters linked to persons, including culture, language policies, education, healthcare, welfare and family policies, and the "regions" (the Flemish region, the Walloon Region and the Region Brussels), on the other hand, responsible for matters linked to territory, like regional economic development, employment, industrial restructuring, environment, land use planning, urban renewal, road building, traffic, agriculture, and export promotion. As concerns the geographic boundaries of these two separate types of federalised units they are only partially identical. A fourth important Belgian peculiarity compared to other federal states is that there is *no hierarchy of standards* between national or federal law on the one hand and community or regional law (decrees or ordinances) on the other hand. Therefore, a community decree on education, for example, can cancel or amend an earlier national law without the national legislator being able to do anything against it, since this matter has been wholly transferred to the communities. If there arise any conflicts of interest they are dealt with by the Court of Arbitration, a kind of Constitutional Court, for legislative acts (bills) and by the Council of State for executive or administrative acts. Finally, the fifth particularity has to be found in the fact that the judicial power remains centralised on the national level. The sub-national entities, Communities and Regions, do not have any responsibility for judicial matters.

Even after the process of state reform, the local level of government remains almost unchanged. On the local level, two levels have to be differentiated, the 10 provinces and the 589 municipalities. The provinces are in charge of local aspects and implementation of educational policy, social services, economic development, culture and recreation, whereas the responsibility of the municipalities is rather vaguely defined by the reference to aspects of local interests.

2.3 Germany

The German system of cooperative federalism is characterised by two basic features. As concerns the distribution of competencies, it is organised along functional lines. While the federal government is in charge of the main fields of legislation, the implementation of national laws is regularly the task of the sixteen Länder administrations. Indeed, there have remained only few exclusive legislative competencies at Länder level not at least due to the extensive federal use of fields of concurrent legislation enumerated in the German constitution, the Basic Law (BL) *("Grundgesetz")*. On the other hand, and this is the second special quality of German federalism, the Länder governments were quite successful in successively widening the scope of federal-level legislation which needs their consent via the Bundesrat. This comprehensive right of legislative codetermination at the federal level and the large degree of discretion in implementing (most) federal laws implies an extraordinarily strong position of the Länder governments compared to the regional level in the other EU Member States. Furthermore, since the introduction of the new Article 23 into the Basic Law in December 1992, the Länder involvement in European policy-making at national level via the Bundesrat is comparable to their strong right of codetermination in domestic policy-making. One result of this fundamental upgrading of their role in European policy-making is that the Länder have played an important role during the preparatory phase of the Intergovernmental conferences of Amsterdam and Nice.

Apparently, the German system of cooperative federalism is highly dependent on the formulation of common Länder interests in the Bundesrat. German unification in 1990, however, entailed an increasing divergence of interests due to the considerable socio-economic disparities between the "old" Länder in West Germany and the "new" Länder" in East Germany. This growing heterogeneity has heavily impaired the smooth operation of joint-decision making *("Politikverflechtung")* at the federal level and first symptoms of institutional gridlock cannot be denied any longer. In addition, the aim of equal living conditions proclaimed by the Basic Law and the system of inter-state financial equalisation have brought a considerable increase of financial burdens for the richer Länder. Due to these recent developments, the current system of financial equalisation and the highly centralised distribution of legislative powers have triggered criticism primarily from the five net contributors among the richer German Länder. As a consequence, there has been a lively reform discussion in Germany since the second half of the 1990s as to whether the legislative and financial autonomy of the Länder should be strengthened and the system of "cooperative federalism" should be transformed into a system of "competitive federalism".

Directly elected assemblies and mayors form the local tier of government. The principle of local self-rule for all matters of local interest is included in the German Constitution in art. 28. With this legally set framework, there is a strong support for local self-rule in the political practice.

3. Country Profiles of Regionalised EU Member States

3.1 France

From 1982 ("Loi Deferre") to 1992 ("Loi Joxe-Marchand") a number of laws were adopted by the French government which have decentralised this EU Member State by creating the institutional framework for the new intermediary level of the 22 "régions" (and 4 overseas regions), devolving a number of competencies to this newly established regional level and by re-arranging the tasks of the local level that consists of the "départements" and the "communes"[3]. Originally, the transfer of powers should be realised by so-called "packages of competencies" for the different territorial authorities in order to avoid splitting up tasks between different levels. In practice, however, this clear-cut distribution of competencies could not be realised and the territorial authorities fulfil voluntary tasks outside their explicit competencies as well. The national level is still the only level with legislative power and remains an important actor with regard to the implementation of laws at regional level. For that purpose, there exist numerous state agencies at regional level, which are coordinated by the prefects as representatives of the central state appointed for each region. These decentralised bodies of the French state exist beside the institutions of the regions, i.e. the regional council, the president of the regional council, and the regional economic and social committee. Therefore, a number of mixed powers, parallel or even competing competencies have emerged and the relation between the levels is characterised by various forms of joint decision-making. The main competencies of the regions are spatial planning and regional economic development including vocational training and research and technology promotion. Furthermore, the regions take share in General Training Policy (as they are in charge of the lycées) and transport policy. The départements are in charge of social aid, public health, school transport, parts of the general training policy (collèges), regional road infrastructure, rural development, environmental protection and sports. The communes as local level of government are in charge of urban

---

[3] As already mentioned above (Footnote 2), the communes, departments and regions are on the same level, according to the French constitutional law. All three subnational entities are qualified as "pouvoirs locaux". Taking a political science perspective and analysing the political practice, it seems however more appropriate to characterise the regions as regional or intermediate level.

development, local infrastructure, housing, public services, social actions, leisure activities and parts of the educational policies (primary level).

As concerns the local level, many of the 36,621 French municipalities are comparatively small and do not dispose of the personal, administrative and financial resources to make use of their increased autonomy resulting from the recent decentralisation process. Plans for a communal reform have failed so far. The 100 departments (existing since the French Revolution) have received important competencies especially in the social and health sector during decentralisation. Compared to the "regions", there is more room for manoeuvre in policy-making for the municipalities and departments as the "classical" territorial authorities in the French system of public administration since they are much better equipped with financial resources than the regions.

With respect to the financial resources, 42% of the sub-national finances are made up of own resources, whereas the rest is provided by resources transferred by the national level (29%), loans, fees and others.

3.2 Italy

The Italian Constitution of 1946 has foreseen the creation of regions from the beginning; but it was not until 1972 that the fifteen regions with "ordinary statute" were really created as sub-national entities. These regions are very restricted in their legislative competencies and are subject to a strong national supervision. Only the five "special statute" regions have some exclusive legislative competencies.

At the beginning of the 1990s a strong tendency towards federalism could be observed in Italy within the context of a broader institutional reform process. In summer 1998, however, the envisaged constitutional reform failed. Important reasons for the failure of the reform were that political players could not agree on the federalisation of the state, disagreed on the future structure of the judicial system and other factors in the reform process. Since then there has been a standstill concerning the further federalisation or regionalisation of the country.

In March 2001, a constitutional law concerning the territorial structure of Italy has been approved. Especially article 117 of the constitution has been changed introducing the principle that regions have legislative powers with reference to all matters that are not explicitly attributed to the national government. The regions have concurrent legislative powers concerning several policy areas. These are especially police matters, public services, public health, vocational training, museums, libraries, local transport infrastructure and others. In these areas, the regions are competent to exercise legislative power within the framework of the legislation and norms set by the national government and while taking account of the national interest. Furthermore, the administrative autonomy of the local authorities is strengthened (according to the reformed article 118 of the constitution). With this reform, Italy is moving from a regional state structure towards more federal structures of state organisation. However, the political consequences of this shift remains to be seen in the political practice[4].

---

[4] In October 2001 a referendum was held on the law agreed upon in March 2001, which covers the reform of the territorial structure of Italy. The constitutional reform has been approved by 64.2% of the voters.

For several reasons there are considerable disparities between the regions in Italy: the northern regions are very close to the centre of Europe, not only in geographical terms but also in terms of economic development whereas the southern regions belong to the periphery position of Europe and are economically underdeveloped. This north-south cleavage is a quite strong determinant in Italian politics.

The local level in Italy consists of the 100 provinces (plus 2 autonomous provinces with special competencies) and the municipalities. Although, the responsibilities of these local bodies are all-embracing within their boundaries according to constitutional theory, national legislation and particularly the explicit transfer of specific tasks to the regional level have restricted provincial activities to a few fields like protection of the environment and the landscape, hunting, fisheries, and road construction. The responsibilities of the municipalities cover primarily land-use planning, local public services and schools. Both levels share tasks related to social welfare, public health, and the operation of hospitals.

3.3 Portugal

Portugal has been a centralised political system for a long time not only in terms of its legal system but also in terms of its system of public administration. Yet, it is has to be classified as a regionalised state since there are the island groups of the Azores and Madeira, which constitute two "Autonomous Regions" with their own governments and legislative assemblies endowed with considerable powers. These autonomous regions do not have own constitutions, as it is known for sub-national entities in federal states, but specific statutes, which regulate their special status and political autonomy. The island regions are competent for all areas of specific regional interest, as for example regional economic development, and aspects related to their specific status as islands remote from the mainland. Furthermore, the island regions possess consultation rights for all matters affecting the regions. Recently, there have been efforts for further regionalisation of continental Portugal by establishing the administrative regions which the Constitution dating back to 1976 provided for from the beginning, but which have never been realised due to strong domestic opposition. However, the proposal to introduce elected regional assemblies at this intermediary level was subject to a referendum and the majority of the Portuguese people finally rejected this plan in November 1998. As a consequence, the 18 districts remain the most important intermediary bodies between the local government and the national level with regard to the mainland – despite their generally weak competencies and the complete lack of any legislative powers. Their tasks are limited to the maintenance of public order, the conduction of elections and the monitoring of the performance of local government. The districts do not even function as administrative bodies. As a result territorial divisions of national ministries carry out most of the central government's activities.

The local tier in Portugal comprises the 4,241 smaller parishes (freguesias) and the 308 municipalities (municípios). The principle of local self-government is included into the Portuguese constitution. Due to their small numbers of inhabitants and their restricted financial resources, the parishes do not play an important role in Portugal. They are responsible for a very few tasks like the promotion of tourism and the local supply of public services. This differs considerably from the role of the 275 municipalities, which have regained a substantial share of autonomy during the decentralisation process since 1976 and are considered today as the most important territorial entities of continental Portugal. They fulfil important administrative functions transferred to them by the national government, especially in the fields of energy supply and waste disposal, public housing and road construction, public transport, sports and culture, local landscape protection and public health.

3.4 Spain

Since the restoration of parliamentary democracy in Spain in 1978 there has been a substantial decentralisation based on the creation of the 17 Autonomous Communities as new regional tier of government. The provinces and municipalities formed the bases for a two-tier structure of local administration prior to 1978. The development of the Autonomous Communities has been a gradual process and has proceeded at an uneven pace. There are two basic types of Autonomous Communities, those with 'high' and those with 'low' responsibilities. The main difference in the range of responsibilities between the two groups has been the assignment of responsibilities in health and education policy to the Autonomous Communities with high responsibilities. The Autonomous Communities possess own, constitutional taxation rights, as they are competent for levying surcharges on national taxes. However, the Spanish regions have decided not to impose additional taxes and remain dependent on resources transferred to them by the national level.

The functions of the central government, Autonomous Communities, provinces and municipalities are not sharply separated, and they are overlapping to a considerable degree. Education and health services are assigned to some but not all of the Autonomous Communities, and are otherwise in the responsibility of the centre. Responsibility for housing, roads and transport, welfare services and economic development is divided between the centre, the Autonomous Communities and, in some cases, the provinces whilst responsibilities for community services, local transport, and sports and cultural facilities is divided between all three levels of sub-central government.

As regards the tasks of the municipalities at the local level, they vary according to the size of their populations. All municipalities have to carry out some compulsory functions in fields like the provision of street lighting, sewage, refuse collection, water supply, road constructing, cemeteries, while larger cities are required to supply a wider range of public services and also share responsibilities with the regional government in the areas of education and public health.

With respect to the political evolution of the regional structure in Spain it needs to be emphasized that it is strongly motivated by important tendencies for regional autonomy and a still ongoing, open process of deconcentration.

3.5 United Kingdom

The United Kingdom has traditionally been viewed as a centralised, unitary state, albeit one practising asymmetric administrative devolution. With the 1997 election of Blair's New Labour government committed to (asymmetrical) devolution, significant changes in the territorial politics of the United Kingdom are underway. Regionalised political structures have been introduced for Scotland, Wales and Northern Ireland, whereas the central government established decentralised tiers of government and non-departmental, public bodies in England.

The devolution of power and political responsibility to the sub-national level follows an asymmetric pattern. For that purpose, a differentiation is made between primary and secondary legislative power. Primary legislative power includes the principle competency for the respective policy field, whereas secondary legislative power refers to the power of defining the way, in which national legislation is implemented in the region.

A Scottish Executive and Scottish Parliament have been established with primary legislative powers in devolved matters plus some tax-raising powers. Scotland's legislative and executive power includes economic development, education and training, environment, transport, local government, social work, health, housing, law and home affairs, agriculture, fisheries and forestry, sport and arts.

Furthermore a National Assembly for Wales with secondary legislative powers has been introduced. Wales possesses only secondary legislative power, which implies a closer supervision of the national level, on the policy areas of economic development, agriculture, forestry, fishery and food, industry and training, education, local government, health and social services, housing, environment, planning, transport, arts, culture, the protection of the Welsh language, built heritage, sport and recreation.

For Northern Ireland, a Northern Ireland Assembly and an Executive has been set up. The Northern Ireland Assembly and Executive has political responsibility for the policy fields of higher education, training, employment, enterprises, trade and investment, regional and social development as well as environment.

In the nine English regions, the central government under John Major set up government offices for the regions in 1994, which serve as platform to deliver a wide range of policies in the regions. The government offices for the regions integrate the activities of various ministries in a single organisation and take over various tasks in the policy implementation and the management of governmental programmes. The governmental offices of the regions are funded and staffed by seven departments of the central government. In 2001, the government offices continued to accumulate further responsibilities, while certain other tasks are transferred to other regional agencies. In the current reform discussion, it has for example been proposed to transfer the competencies for Public Health Policy implementation in England to the government offices. In addition to the government offices, regional chambers have been established in the English regions, which fulfil an advisory function. They are concerned with regional affairs and seek to improve communication and public awareness. The regional chambers have received own financial resources in order to carry out collective projects. The regional assemblies bring together elected representatives of the local authorities and other regional partners in a forum for issues of shared interest. With these regional assemblies, the regional accountability shall be strengthened. The regional assemblies are therefore another example of the ongoing process of devolution in the United Kingdom. The political role and tasks of the regional assemblies are, however, vaguely defined and still evolving. Therefore, these chambers have not been included in the tabular overviews on the five policy fields examined in this study.

Furthermore appointed Regional Development Agencies began operating in England in 1999. The eight Regional Development Agencies (RDA) in England are non-departmental public bodies, accountable to ministers through a corporate planning process and responsive to their local communities. The RDAs consist of twelve members appointed by ministers and drawn from a variety of backgrounds including business, local authorities, education and the voluntary sector. The RDAs in England do not have the power to make legislation or regulations, or the power to fix fees or charges. Their main task is to contribute to the policies and programmes on transport, land use, environment and sustainable development, education, public health, housing, tourism, culture, sport and infrastructure projects. Since 2001, the RDAs are in charge of the administration of the EU Structural Funds for England. With the extension of their tasks, the financial and administrative resources have been extended. The Regional Development Agencies are required to take account of the views of the regional chambers in formulating their strategy and policy for the region.

Beside the asymmetric devolution in Scotland, Wales and Northern Ireland and the transfer of administrative tasks to the English regions and RDA, also the local level of government has been reformed. In 1998, the White Paper "Modern Local Government: In Touch with the People", set out a strategy for the reform of local government in England. In Scotland 32 unitary authorities were created to replace the previous two-tier system of local government in 1996. In Wales, the government for the reform of local government overtook the proposals of the White Paper. The local government is generally based on a statute and derives its power from legislation. The local governments in the UK, which are elected directly, undertake a wide range of actions related to local affairs, however similar to the local tiers of government in the other Member States.

These recent and current decentralisation and regionalisation processes are still the subject of political discussion.

4. Country Profiles of Decentralised EU Member States

4.1 Denmark

In Denmark there are three territorial levels of government: the national level, the regional level consisting of fourteen counties (amter) and the local level with its 270 municipalities (kommuner). Between the regional and local levels of government, there is no clear-cut hierarchy and both levels are closely interrelated and interlocked. Local autonomy is governed by statute. Nominally, there is no "regional" level of government. What in the Danish context would qualify as "regional", however, is the special regime that has been set up for the Faeroe Islands and Greenland including far-reaching autonomy and home rule. Domestic affairs are decentralised and the counties and municipalities administer 70 % of total public expenditure.

The county level carries out functions that are too comprehensive to be handled by the local authorities, as for example in the field of public health where the counties are responsible for hospitals and other facilities of health care. Furthermore, the counties are endowed with the competencies for public transport at the regional level, high school education, and vocational training as well as with numerous tasks in the field of environment.

The Danish municipalities are primarily responsible for supplying public services, primary and lower secondary schools, the administration of social benefits, local road construction and local public transport, housing and urban planning, water quality, waste disposal.

However the coordination of policies is very centralised. There is a certain dilemma between the wish that the municipalities should decide as much as possible on their own and the wish that the citizens are treated equally and receive the same standard of services all over Denmark. Despite well developed levels of government, Denmark remains relatively centralised as the guidelines for policy making are drawn up at national level, and the national level also ensures that the municipalities and the counties meet demands.

4.2 Finland

As in many other EU Member States, some administrative functions in Finland were devolved to lower tiers of government in the 1990s. In 1990 many functions were transferred to the municipalities and special regional units; for example, responsibility for environmental issues was transferred to the regional environmental agencies. In addition, new regional bodies, called regional councils, were set up. The regional councils draw up regional development programmes together with the relevant municipalities, central government authorities, industry and commerce, and NGOs. They also participate in management of EU aid. The administrative functions of central government administration at regional level are carried out by the provincial state offices, which are controlled and supervised by the Ministry of the Interior. There are six provinces. The provinces are part of central government administration and they were established in 1997 to replace the former 12 provinces. There are no democratically elected bodies in the provinces. The Employment and Economic Development Centres are also part of central government administration at regional level.

The municipalities are the basic units at local level, and the principle of municipal self-government is enshrined in the Finnish Constitution. The municipalities' overall function, the provision of public services for their inhabitants, is based on this principle. Consequently, municipalities are entitled to levy taxes on their inhabitants in order to provide services. Central government passively supervises the legality of municipal activities.

4.3 The Netherlands

The Netherlands is a decentralised state with three levels of government: central government, the provinces at regional level and the municipalities at local government.

The municipalities are responsible for a wide range of public service tasks. These tasks are carried out under the system of joint activities whereby the central government lays down the legal framework for the municipal activities through detailed regulations. However, the municipalities hold a certain degree of autonomy in some areas. The policy fields are not determined by policy areas, but corresponding to their nature and the limitations resulting from the size of the municipalities and the limits set by fundamental rights and the principle of consociational democracy, a limiting factor also applicable for the scope of action of the provinces. Furthermore, the municipalities possess the right of appeal to the courts and the Council of State.

Beside the municipalities, the 12 provinces form the second tier of sub-national government. With respect to the degree of autonomy, there exists the same relation to the national government as for the municipalities. The most important provincial activities are traffic and public transport, welfare services, town and country planning and environmental protection. In general, they perform activities that are complicated and technically demanding and therefore require an administrative capacity, which is not available in the average municipality. Besides these activities, the provinces have a general role in the advancement of inter-municipal cooperation of supra-local activities. In some fields (e.g. town and country planning, municipal budgets) the provinces supervise the municipalities, though in day-to-day practice this formal task is marginalized in comparison with mutual consultation, assistance and cooperation.

4.4 Sweden

Sweden is going through a period of decentralisation and regionalisation. The principle of local self-government is included in the Swedish Constitution in the respective chapter on the different instruments of government. At an intermediary level, there are two different bodies at the moment: the county administrative boards which are important as coordinators and controllers of activities and provide the regions with a lot of funding for the regional development as decided by government and parliament; and the elected county councils which are primarily responsible for health care and transport services and some regional development programmes.

On the intermediate level, it is important to differentiate between the two sub-national entities of Landsting and Län, beside the experimental regions, to which we will turn later. The 18 Landsting (County Councils) are a sub-national level of government with an elected County Council Assembly and a County Executive Committee. The County Councils are in charge of public health, public transport, environment, and increasingly certain tasks in the implementation of regional development programmes (especially for those County Councils outside the experimental regions). Further areas of competency are culture and certain aspects of education.

Beside the County Councils there exist 21 Län, which operate as regional administration of the central government. The boards of this sub-national entity consist on the one hand of 15 members for each province, which are elected by the county council, and on the other hand of the county governor, who is nominated by and subordinate to the central government.

This double-tier construction often causes conflicts, especially with regard to regional development.

Additionally, four "experimental" regions have recently been established in Sweden. Some of these regions are composed of more but one county (läns) and enjoy the status of self-governing authorities, which have taken over the responsibility for regional development from the county administrative boards. Moreover, considerable tasks in the fields of transport, culture, tourism and environment have been transferred to them. This experiment was started in 1997 and will last until 2002. During the year 2001, a decision on the prolongation of the programme will be taken. First political discussions indicate a preference for the prolongation of the project on the experimental regions until 2006. This might be a first step towards a regional government structure in accordance with recent developments in the multi-level systems of other EU Member States. However, these experimental regions do not cover the whole territory of Sweden and it remains to be seen if this experiment will be extended over the whole country.

Under the Constitution the local level has a high status in Sweden. The municipalities have a predominant role in the field of public welfare. The 289 municipalities carry out mandatory tasks in social services, vocational training and environmental issues and voluntary tasks in transport policy. Furthermore, they are in charge of aspects of local interest, energy distribution, waste collection, tourism, leisure activities, local economic development, social security, elderly care and others.

With respect to the political relationship between the different levels, it is important to emphasise the following aspects. On the one hand, a considerable amount of public spending is allocated at national level. The strong position of the political parties is a further, integrating factor in political practice. Furthermore, certain tasks are carried out by state regional boards, which do not form a regional level of government, but state administration at the regional level. This is for example the case for regional policy outside the experimental regions. Regarding EU policies, a close interrelation of national policies and the EU agenda can be observed. This has had impact on the intergovernmental relations within Sweden (between the national and sub-national levels of government) since EU membership.

5. *Country Profiles of Two-Tiered EU Member States*

5.1 Greece

Greece has remained a strongly centralised state for a long time. Until 1994, municipal and town councils represented the only elected bodies below the national level. The 51 prefectures were decentralised units of central government, which enabled the national government to control the local level. The prefects were appointed by the national government. In 1994, however, elected prefectural councils and governors were introduced as a second tier of local self-government, which are in charge of the economic, social and cultural development at regional level. This reform constituted a major adaptation of the system. Since then, also the prefect is elected directly. Since the end of the 1980s, local government structures are in a process of change and adaptation, which has led to greater local autonomy, especially in fiscal terms, within the centralised structure of the Greek system.

13 regions have been established since 1987 as new tier of regional administration as a response to the EU Regional and Structural Policy. The regions are decentralised tiers of the national government, however, without own policy responsibility and strictly subordinate to the national government. Main tasks of the regional level are the programming, planning and coordination of regional development, which is fulfilled by non-elected regional councils. The secretary general of the region supervises the activities of the prefects.

Due to the far-reaching supervision by the central government, their extremely restricted financial resources and the lack of financial autonomy, the responsibilities of Greek municipalities are restricted to classical tasks of the local level, like public water supply, waste and sewage disposal, leisure and public parks, local road construction and local public transport and building supervision. But social welfare tasks like childcare, health care or social assistance do not belong to the municipal responsibilities but are provided for either by the church in Greece or – as concerns health care – by the central government.

The municipal level is in charge of regulating local affairs, promote local social and economic interests as well as cultural and intellectual matters.

Since 1995, the process of transferring additional powers to the local level is going on. In order to ensure a smooth transition, however, the central government has chosen a strategy of small successive steps. For that reason, devolution is not completed yet. In the longer run, several matters will fall within the exclusive responsibility of towns and municipalities while more complex matters which go beyond their financial and administrative capacities, like economic and regional planning, shall be transferred to the directly elected prefectural councils, existing since 1994, and the regions. Furthermore, an increased need for defining the exact scope of local affairs is needed, as the different tiers of sub-national levels compete currently for specific tasks. Finally, budgetary and financial aspects of the balance of power need to be regulated, as the transfer of tasks needs to be linked to a transfer of resources and a (however limited) financial independence.

5.2 Ireland

Ireland is geographically divided into the four provinces of Munster, Connaught, Ulster and Leinster, which however fulfil no political or administrative functions. The 26 counties and the five county boroughs of the biggest towns in the Republic, i.e. Dublin, Cork, Limerick, Waterford, and Galway, constitute the next tier at the local level. Since 1991, when the Local Government Act abolished the restrictive rule that activities of local authorities in fields, which are not explicitly transferred to them by national law, are subject to the "ultra vires" doctrine, the counties have become the centre of sub-national political action in Ireland. Below the county level, there are so-called "county borough corporations", "borough corporations", "urban district councils" and "town commissioners" that represent the lowest tier of local government and are concentrated in urban areas. In June 1999, the result of a referendum considerably strengthened the internal role of these Irish local authorities by endowing them with a constitutional status. The County Councils do not enjoy extensive political or fiscal powers but a greater independence can be identified with respect to the implementation and detailed regulation of government policies.

At the regional level, eight regional authorities were established in 1994 in order to coordinate the supply of public services, to promote coordination and cooperation between local authorities and to fulfil an advisory function in the implementation of EU structural funding. In addition, the Irish government created two new regional associations at NUTS II level in 1999. These Regional Assemblies manage the Regional Operational Programmes and monitor the impact of EU programmes in their areas.

With respect to EU policies and the participation of Irish sub-national players, the fields of mandatory consultation have led to a strengthening of the regions and a growing awareness of the regional factor in Ireland.

5.3 Luxembourg

Luxembourg is a small country with no regional tier of government. The 118 municipalities of the Grand Duchy constitute the basic level of local government. In order to guarantee a better coordination between the activities of the central government and the municipalities the country is sub-divided into three districts, which have, however, no executive functions and cannot be considered as a real element of territorial decentralisation for that reason. Due to the size of the country, there are strong links between the central and the local level, for example, many members of the national parliament are at the same time mayors of municipalities.

The main tasks of the municipalities are water supply, sewerage and waste-water treatment, fire services, the provision of social facilities and services like nurseries, kindergartens, care for the elderly, and cultural and leisure activities. In the field of education, they share most responsibilities with the central government. The same holds true for public sector services like road construction and maintenance, refuse collection and disposal. During the last years, the local level has gained some more autonomy vis-à-vis the central level. Nevertheless, the territorial structures of the country are still characterised by a high degree of centralisation as can be illustrated, for example, by the fact that the municipal budget still has to be approved by the Minister of the Interior.

III. Joint Policy-Making in the Maastricht Fields of Mandatory Consultation: Forms of Cooperation and Coordination

1. Systems of Joint-Policy-Making and Multi-Level Governance

Within this chapter of the study, it is the main objective of the research team to give a brief overview on the forms of cooperation between the different levels of government in the EU Member States and the specific forms of Multi-Level Governance.

In political science, the topic of the interaction and cooperation between different levels of government has been subject to scientific research since a considerable time. Some examples of conceptions to analyse both the multi-level character of the policy-making and the interrelation and intersection of different levels of government shall be mentioned here. For the case of Germany and the German federal structure, Fritz Scharpf (1976) has described these forms of interrelation and interaction as joint-decision-trap *("Politikverflechtungsfalle")*. Building on this concept, the participation of the German Länder in the EU policy making process has been analysed and described as multi-level or double joint-decision making *("doppelte Politikverflechtung")*. These concepts lay a focus on the aspect of common, joint-decision-making rather than on the regions or sub-national players acting independently on the community or international level. Within these concepts, the regions are closely interrelated and integrated into the decision-making system of the national political systems. They have the possibility and developed the capacity to take part in the policy formulation and implementation of policies related to the EU and take part in the shaping of the national position within the EU context.

In the 1990s, the participation of sub-national players in the policy making on the EU level has been characterised in a general concept as multi-level-governance (e.g. Marks, 1996). Governance, understood as governmental decisions on binding regulation of specific topics or issues, is, according to this concept, not concentrated on the national level, but located on various levels with different players from the national and / or regional level acting in a specific policy field. These forms of multi-level governance are a typical characteristic of the federal EU Member States. The characteristic of multi-level governance is most visible in the EU Regional and Structural Policy, whereas other policy fields, as for example the policy on the establishment of Transeuropean Networks, are much more determined and dominated by the central government. Within the scientific discourse on multi-level governance, this form of shared and divided policy responsibility has been analysed for several Member States. In these cases, it seems to be justified to characterise the division of competencies also as shared sovereignty. The German Länder as well as the Belgian Communities and Regions, for example, take actively part in the policy making on the European level and act, within their sphere of competency, independently from the national government. This form of multi-level governance is combined with forms of coordination between the regions / communities respectively between the Länder in order to assure the coherence of the policy-making. With respect to the multi-level governance character of the policy-making in the Maastricht Fields of Mandatory Consultation it seems necessary to emphasise that the sub-national level, also presenting a separate level of governance, coordinates its policy making and political strategy mainly along national lines, meaning that for example the German Länder act mainly as coalition and take part in the EU policy making with political objectives and strategies, which were previously agreed between them. Similarly, the cooperation between the Belgian regions and Communities is much more important compared to forms of transnational cooperation on the sub-national level. In general terms, it is justified to underline that the form of multi-level governance is a typical characteristic of many Member States, especially of the federal and regionalised states. The multi-level governance is complimented by differentiated forms of cooperation and coordination both on a specific level of government and between the levels of government. These forms of coordination aim at improving the performance of the various players in the policy process and the policy output.

The organisational framework and political practice is, however, different for the decentralised and two-tiered states. In these states, the form of cooperation takes mainly the form of consultations between the regions and with the national level. The consultation takes place within informal and ad hoc consultations between the entities on the regional and local level as well as with the central government. Only in a limited number of cases, these consultations have evolved into formalised forms of cooperation. Even though these forms of consultation form an essential channel for influencing the national position in the EU negotiations for the regions in decentralised and two-tiered states, these forms are considerably weaker compared to the system of multi-level governance in federal and regionalised states. Similarly, the channels of access are to a lower degree formalised and guaranteed. Cooperation and governance of sub-national players in the fields of mandatory consultation is therefore very closely linked to and interconnected with the share of competencies and policy responsibility within a specific policy field.

By using the forms of cooperation and coordination, the regions aim at influencing and co-determining the national positions in the EU negotiations. The coordination is used as an additional and complementary channel of access, beside other forms of regional or local interest representation in the EU and on the EU level, as the Committee of the Regions, the information offices set up by regions in Brussels and other forms. With this strategy of using various and complementary channels of access, the regions aim at increasing their benefit from European integration (e.g. by a very active role in the policy field of Regional and Structural Policy) and advocate their demands.

2. Federal States

2.1 Austria

General Forms of Cooperation

Within the Austrian political system, there are various forms of formal and informal cooperation and coordination between the different levels of government. The guiding principles and characteristics of these forms of cooperation are similar for all policy fields and specific forms of coordination are used for various policy fields. In this chapter, the research team will first briefly describe or mention these forms of cooperation and afterwards give a political assessment of these developments. The most important form of cooperation between the Länder is the Conference of the Land governors *("Konferenz der Landeshauptmänner")*, which meets twice a year. Within this conference, the governments of the Länder coordinate their policies as far as such a coordination is useful and necessary. Additionally, formal and informal meetings of the ministers of the Länder, as well as of the Länder and the federal level, take place both on an ad-hoc and regular basis. Furthermore, the Länder prepare common positions dealing with European Affairs and agree on political objectives for the negotiations in the Council of Ministers. A constitutional procedure for cooperation on EU affairs as been included in the Austrian constitution in orders to guarantee the participation rights of the sub-national level (Art. 23 a - f).

Policy Field Specific Characteristics

Beside these general forms of cooperation and coordination, specific bodies with coordinating functions have been established for various policy fields. The most important of these is the Austrian Conference of Spatial Planning *("Österreichische Raumordnungskonferenz, ÖROK)*, which serves as coordinating body for regional policy, spatial planning and infrastructure planning, including the participation in TEN projects. For Culture, it is important to emphasize the low degree of coordination, which is characterised by parallel structures on the different levels and a comparatively large freedom of the Länder. The external Cultural Policy is reserved for the federal level. In Public Health, an increased need for coordination can be observed with respect to the planning of public health infrastructure (e.g. hospitals). These aspects are regulated in the Commission for the Public Health Sector *("Strukturkommission für das Gesundheitswesen")*. In the national transport and infrastructure policy, corresponding to TEN, an important role has been assigned to the specialised corporations for motorways *("Autobahn- und Schnellstraßenfinanzierungsaktiengesellschaft")* and the corresponding corporation for the railway sector. Finally, a complex network of cooperation and coordination has been established in the formulation and implementation of Regional and Structural Policy, with all levels taking part in the implementation. A central role in this network has been attributed to the ÖROK, which contributes to improvement of conditions of employment, which supports peripheral, agrarian regions and serves as platform for the coordination of policies affecting regional development. A subcommittee of the ÖROK deals with EU Regional Policy.

2.2 Belgium

General Forms of Cooperation

When analysing the forms of cooperation and coordination in the federal system of Belgium, it is important to emphasize, that the Belgian federal model is much more based on the separation of tasks and responsibilities than other federal states. With the fundamental conflicts in the Belgian society being the central element and driving force in the process leading to the federal structure, the political players aimed at limiting the actual need for cooperation. By reducing the number of areas decided jointly, the Belgian authorities aimed at limiting the potential for political conflicts and a resulting political stalemate.

This general characteristic of separation of task and autonomy does, however, not imply that there are no forms of cooperation and coordination. On the one hand, the Flemish Community and the French

Community cooperate in cultural and general training matters for Brussels in the common community commission. This commission deals with all Brussels-related matters covered by competencies of the Belgian Communities. Coordination between regional and community authorities and local authorities is furthermore taking place in the implementation of programmes, for example in youth policy.

Furthermore, the Belgian Committees and Regions coordinate their policies as far the EU is concerned. Within the Council of Ministers and other EU institutions, the sub-national players in Belgian aim at implementing a joint policy, which is coordinated between the sub-national governments and the joint-Brussels office.

Policy Field Specific Characteristics

Some specific tendencies in the field of cooperation and coordination for the Maastricht fields of Mandatory CoR consultation should additionally be mentioned. In Culture, the actual need and practice of coordination is apparently rather limited. The general coordination takes place mainly on an informal basis or in the procedures for EU affairs. The need for cooperation is significantly higher in Public Health, as the competencies of the federal, regional and community level are much more interrelated in this area. The different national and sub-national players cooperate in the formulation and implementation of various, specific aspects of Public Health. In the policy field of Regional and Structural Policy, coordination takes only place as far as the participation in EU programmes is concerned. The national policies for regional development fall completely under the authority of the respective region. Within the regions, area platforms have been established, composed of delegates from the municipalities, social partners and political parties.

2.3 Germany

General Forms of Cooperation

As regards the cooperation between the Länder, important general forms of cooperation have to be mentioned, which apply to all policy fields. These are the cooperation between the Länder in the federal chamber *("Bundesrat")*, which serves as coordinating institution for common positions for the CoR. In this respect, it is, however, important to emphasise that the German local representatives within the CoR do not take part in this coordination mechanism. A further form of coordination between the Länder is the conference of ministers for European affairs, which deals also with all policy fields. The conference aims at coordinating the position of the Länder for a common interest representation in the EU institutions, including the CoR.

Finally, the cities and municipalities have set up institutions of cooperation and joint-interest representation ("Deutscher Städtetag" / "Deutscher Städte- und Gemeindebund").

Policy Field Specific Characteristics

Coordination and the policy making in the cooperative federalism is a typical feature of the German political system. The form of policy making has led to a wide range and intensive network of coordination for various policy fields. In the context of this study, the research team has decided to illustrate the coordination, by taking the coordination in the context of the General Training and Youth Policy and Culture as an example. A typical example of such a highly institutionalised form of cooperation between the Länder is the conference of cultural ministers *("Kultusministerkonferenz")*, which deals both with cultural and general training matters. The conference of cultural ministers has been established in 1946 and decides on a consensual basis. It is a typical example of the German cooperative federal system. However, coordination and political exchange is not only taking place on a ministerial level, but in a large number of working groups and consultative and cooperative institutions on the administrative level.

3. Regionalised States

3.1 France

General Forms of Cooperation

Coordination takes on the one hand place on an inter-ministerial base. Furthermore, central, regional and local authorities and administrations coordinate their policies in various sectors. The prefect, acting as state representative on the sub-national level, fulfils a major, coordinating function.

Policy Field Specific Characteristics

The distribution of competencies in the policy field of General Training and Youth has led to a complex network of responsibilities and an increased need for cooperation between the different levels. Cooperation and coordination is taking place mainly on an ad-hoc and informal basis. General

Training policy can be identified as the policy field with the most visible sub-national influence. A significant, informal influence on the policy shaping has been attributed to the mayors in General Training and Youth. In the policy shaping of Youth policy, the local authorities have considerable freedom. In Public Health, the prefect fulfils an important role in the administration of public health commissions, health services and the coordination of health programmes. Furthermore, the regional and local level have set up conferences for specific policy fields, as for example the conference on Public Health, which fixes regional priorities for Public Health and develops public health programmes. The infrastructure policy and the projects comparable to TEN are still treated as rather national matter with only limited possibilities for setting priorities on the regional and local level. The prefect as representative of the state has a strong position in the project implementation. In Regional and Structural Policy, an important, coordinating role is attributed to the General Secretariat for Regional Affairs (DATAR, délégation à l'aménagement du territoire et à l'action régionale), which acts as coordinating institution for regional policy and spatial planning since 1963.

3.2 Italy

General Form of Cooperation

The joint Conference between regions and National Government (Conferenza Stato-Regioni) discusses all matters related to EU affairs, serves as forum for the information exchange and prepares common positions of the Italian regions. In its reunions, further meetings are held from time to time including regional representatives and representatives from the national government. In these reunions, the regional and national level coordinate their common positions on European Affairs. The state-regional conference serves as formalised form of coordination between the state and the regions. Additionally, the different levels of government exchange their view and cooperate on an informal basis.

Policy Field Specific Characteristics

Beside these general forms of coordination and cooperation certain specific characteristics of the policy fields examined in this study have to be mentioned. For General Training, it is important to emphasize the unitarian character of the school system and the regional focus on higher education and school education. When assessing the political influence of the different levels of government in the policy field of General Training, a dominant position of the central government can be identified. In Youth policy, the local level is particular active and Youth policy can be characterised as the policy field with the most visible local influence. Local authorities have set up youth institutions and centres, covering a wide range of policy objectives and youth policy activities. In the area of Culture, a wide range of activities is developed on the regional level. The sub-national authorities have set up various forms of cultural institutions. However, the national level has an influential role on the overall shaping of Culture and is the most important level with respect to EU and external Cultural Policy. The policy field of Public Health is the area with the most visible influence and responsibility of the regions. The regions have a leading position in this policy, without the need of cooperation with national government. In the policies on the establishment of Transeuropean Networks, the national level is in a dominant position and the sub-national level has only informal channels of access. However, a major interest of the regions in this policy field has been identified. For the cooperation and coordination in Regional and Structural Policy, two programming levels have to be differentiated (national and regional). On the national level, a National Committee of European Structural Funds has been set up as central planning body. The regional planning has to be approved by central level. However, the regions have *de lege* and *de facto* a significant influence on the policy shaping and the distribution of funds. Additionally, the regions have established informal contacts with the EU Commission, which are, in certain cases, stronger than with national level. Of the total volume of the regional funding provided by the EU for Italy, 88% are directly transferred to the regions, 12% remains on the national level for interregional programmes.

3.3 Portugal

General Forms of Cooperation

In Portugal, the cooperation between the central government and regional and local authorities takes mainly the form of consultation agreements. Cooperation and coordination is furthermore taking place between the administrations involved and in formalised working groups. The sub-national, political influence within these forms of consultation and cooperation is, however, rather limited.

The most important informal channel of political access is the lobbying of the members of parliament of the respective region. By informing the parliamentarians about the local needs and demands, local authorities are able to exercise considerable, sub-national pressure and influence. Cooperation between the national government and administration and the local authorities is furthermore taking place in the implementation of concrete projects (financial participation, programming contracts).

Policy Field Specific Characteristics

Beside these general forms of coordination, certain central features of the five policy fields related to the coordination between the different levels shall be mentioned. For General Training and Youth, the regional and local authorities increasingly perceive institutions for General Training as important factor for the regional development. In Youth Policy, the Secretary General for Youth serves as coordinating body and administrative tasks are fulfilled by the Institute of Youth, which has set up regional departments. In Culture, central and local authorities cooperate in the setting up and running of museums, financial support is provided for various cultural activities. In the political practice, considerable differences can be observed with respect to the scope and kind of the cultural activities. A major role in the implementation and shaping of Culture is attributed to the national Gulbenkian Foundation. Public Health and Transeuropean Networks are mainly national policies, determined by the central government, in which the regional and local authorities take part in consultative procedures and by programming contracts. In Regional and Structural Policy, formal and informal cooperation is taking place between the different levels as well as between the local level and the EU. Furthermore, the local level is involved in transnational, regional cooperation as the European Networks of cities, Eurometropolis and the Atlantic Arch.

3.4 Spain

General Forms of Cooperation

For European Affairs, general consultations between the central level and the Autonomous Communities take place in a rather formalised procedure. Further forms of cooperation include certain regions (e.g. Catalonia) and the central government. The Conference for affairs related to the EU (including representatives from each region and the national level) deals with various EU affairs. A specialised Committee deals with the EU affairs on a day-to-day basis. These forms of cooperation and coordination apply to all policy fields. Personal ties and relations have a comparatively strong influence on the relationship between the different levels of government in Spain. The political influence of the Autonomous Communities varies considerably, depending on their political capacities, leadership and financial resources.

Policy Field Specific Characteristics

In addition to the forms of cooperation mentioned above, Spanish regions cooperate with other regions, for example in the framework of the "Four Motors for Europe (Baden-Württemberg, Lombardy, Rhone-Alpes, Catalonia), which serves as basis for joint interest representation. Beside these general forms of coordination and cooperation, some characteristics of certain policy fields shall be mentioned in this section. It has already been said in the chapter on the country profile on Spain, that the AC can accede different degrees of autonomy. General Training Policy is a typical example for differentiated degrees of autonomy, as certain competencies for regulating matters of General Training have only been transferred to the those AC, which are mentioned in art. 151 of the Spanish Constitution (Andalusia, Canary Islands, Catalonia, Galicia, the Basque Country, Navarra and Valencia). In the area of Culture, the AC's are increasingly involved in trans-frontier cultural cooperation, sometimes making use of the INTERREG framework. In Public Health, cooperation between the different levels is taking place on specific topics, as for example drug prevention (with a national plan on drug addiction and specific regional plans on the AC level). In Regional and Structural Policy, additional cooperation is stimulated and encouraged by the European Commission in the context of the application of the principle of partnership. An active participation and involvement in the EU regional policy can especially be identified for those AC with a higher status of autonomy. However, considerable differences exist between the AC's with respect to the scope and intensity of their participation in Regional and Structural Policy.

3.5 United Kingdom

General Forms of Cooperation

The general procedures of cooperation and coordination between the central government and the devolved administrations in the UK are almost exclusively of informal character. However, a process towards more formalised structures of cooperation can be observed in recent years. A general procedure of consultation and cooperation between the central and regional level has been established for European affairs, with specialised rules for a number of policy fields. Additionally, a close network of informal cooperation has been established on working group level.

Policy Field Specific Characteristics

In a number of policy fields, further, specific coordinating mechanisms between the different levels of government have been established. In the field of Culture, for example, the national government implements an arm-length approach by providing financial means for non-departmental, public bodies (e.g. the Arts Council for England or public museums), while not leaving considerable freedom for those being active in Culture. As the political responsibility in Public Health is shared between the different levels, there is an intensive need and actual practice of cooperation, which has led to specific forms of coordination and cooperation. In Public Health, a pattern of formal joint-policy making has evolved. The National Health Service is cooperating in a partnership with the local authorities. The political players of the different levels are supported by a large number of specialised, advisory committees (e.g. Expert Advisory Group on AIDS). Since 2000, a national Health Development Agency has been set up in England, which aims at improving public health. In the policy on Transeuropean Networks, the Highway Agency, which operates as executive agency of the national department, serves as specialised, coordinating body beside the general forms of coordination and cooperation.

Additionally, agencies and councils have been established for the coordination of specific policies and programmes (e.g. for training and exchange programmes; Socrates Erasmus Council, Scottish Higher Education Funding Council, Scottish Education Council, Scottish Student Awards Agency).

4. Decentralised States

4.1 Denmark

General Forms of Cooperation

In Denmark, the Association of County Councils serves as general forum for the policy coordination and cooperation between the national level and the local authorities. Especially with respect to the participation of the regions in EU programmes and the EU policies, the Association of County Councils fulfils an important role. Additionally, the County Councils take part in interregional cooperations, while using the existing networks (e.g. INTERREG).

Policy Field Specific Characteristics

Further aspects of cooperation and coordination are related to specific policy fields. In General Training and Youth, for example, boards and user councils are a significant element of coordination. In General Training and Youth policy, the principle of self-management and self-rule applies. Municipalities and County Councils may and often do pass over their responsibilities to these boards. For the national Youth Policy, a Youth Council has been set up, which fulfils coordination tasks.

In the policies corresponding to TEN, national agencies have a fundamental role in the policy shaping and implementation. Coordination is to a lesser extent formalised between the national level and the local authorities, but between distinct bodies on the national level. The county councils as well as the local authorities make intensive use of the informal channels of political access, as for example the lobbying on the participation in TEN projects.

In Regional and Structural Policy, the regional authorities have an important function. The sub-national participation in the policy process is explicitly welcomed and promoted by the European institutions, especially in the context of the principle of partnership. Regional and Structural Policy in Denmark is more and more implemented in a bottom-up approach. A specialised, national agency fulfils additional tasks of coordination and implementation of the Danish participation in the EU Regional and Structural Policy.

4.2 Finland

General Forms of Cooperation

As for the other Member States already analysed, also for Finland certain, general forms of coordination and cooperation can be identified, which are complemented by specific characteristics of certain policy fields.

The general coordination between the municipalities is taking place in the Association of Municipalities. It serves further more as coordinating institution between the national and local level. Similarly, the regional councils have set up procedures for the policy coordination on the regional level. A further, separate coordination and consultation procedure has been established for EU affairs, which deals with all EU policies affecting the regional and local level.

Policy Field Specific Characteristics

Turning from these general forms of coordination to specific characteristics of the policy fields examined in this study, the following aspects have to be mentioned. In General Training and Youth policy, a specifically high importance of coordination is a major characteristic of the policy field. By using this coordination, the quality of the educational services shall be improved. For Culture, the Arts Council has been set up as coordinating body, which is in charge of the allocation of grants. The Arts Council of Finland has set up regional branches, which promote arts and artistic activities. In Public Health, cooperation and coordination is taking place between the municipalities in the service provision, especially with respect to the specialised care. In the policy on the establishment of Transeuropean Networks, the cooperation between the different levels of government is not very well developed and only to a limited extent formalised. Regional and local authorities use mainly informal channels of access for influencing the policy field. In the Regional and Structural Policy, the Regional Councils fulfil an important, coordinating function. The Regional Councils are in charge of setting objectives, develop strategies and regional development programmes. The cooperation between the regional authorities and the national government takes place mainly on an informal basis. In order to support the regional development, the Centres of Expertise Programme has been set up. The 14 Regional Centres promote the information exchange, support the use of information technology, job creation and regional development.

4.3 The Netherlands

General Forms of Cooperation

In The Netherlands, the general coordination and cooperation on the local level is taking place in the Association of Municipalities. It serves furthermore as forum for common interest representation on the EU level and coordinates the cooperation with the national government. In Regional and Structural Policy, the coordinating role is to a certain extend transferred from the national Ministry of the Interior to the Association of Municipalities.

Policy Field Specific Characteristics

Additionally further, specific aspects have to be mentioned for the five policy fields examined in this study. For General Training and Youth, informal cooperation seems to be of higher importance than the formal cooperation. The local authorities are involved in the formulation and implementation of concrete projects on General Training. Within the policy field, a significant influence of consociational principles is a central characteristic, which has led to a more influential role of the national government. The political role and autonomy of the sub-national authorities is rather limited in General Training, whereas the local level implements a more active role in Youth Policy. However, it is important to emphasize that Youth Policy is equally rooted in the Dutch consociational democracy. In Culture, public activities concentrate on the provision of financial support and on the regulation of financial aspects. Cooperation between the different levels is implemented within the framework of financial commitments of the central government. The political influence of the national level is comparatively high, especially with respect to the informal cooperation. In the policy formulation of Public Health, the political role of the sub-national level is rather limited. The national administration and government cooperates with the local authorities in the planning of public health facilities and priorities. Cooperation is taking place for the on-the-spot distribution and allocation of means. In the policy implementation, the sub-national level fulfils an important function and takes part in the policy shaping. In the national policies corresponding the TEN, the sub-national level is in weak position, as major infrastructure projects are planned and implemented by the national level. The state has a monopoly in the planning phase of these major transport infrastructure projects. Sub-national cooperation on infrastructure projects is taking place in the context of interregional cooperation agreements (e.g. Euroregio Rijn-Waal), activities, which are, however, not covered by the EU policies on Transeuropean Networks. In Regional and Structural Policy, a close network of coordinating institutions has been established. A Regional Development Agency has been set up by the national government, which operates on the regional level. Furthermore, public sector institutions (e.g. public agencies) take part in the shaping and implementation of regional development policies. In the political practice, the central government answers regional demands, especially with respect to the EU Regional and Structural Policies. The distribution and "handing out" of financial support remains under the authority of the national government. The programmes related to the ESF are completely within the authority of the national level. However, the sub-national authorities use increasingly informal channels for influencing the policy making on regional development and policies related to the ESF, especially by lobbying the national and EU institutions.

4.4 Sweden

General Forms of Cooperation

On the level of general forms of cooperation and coordination, two institutions are of major importance, which are the Association of Local Authorities and the Federation of County Councils. Common positions of the local authorities both for the national political negotiations with the central government and for the EU policies are negotiated and coordinated within these associations.

Policy Field Specific Characteristics

Beside these general forms of cooperation, some specific characteristics of the policy fields examined shall be mentioned. In General Training and Youth, cooperation is implemented in cooperation agreements between the different levels of government. Furthermore, the National Agency for Education fulfils policy coordinating tasks. The structures of coordination established are highly flexible and follow a bottom-up rethinking of General Training Policy. For Youth Policy, a network for cooperation has been established. Furthermore, the Assembly of Swedish Youth Organisations takes part in the policy shaping and coordination. In Culture, the National Council for Cultural Affairs is the coordinating body for the administration of grants. Coordination and Cooperation is also a typical characteristic of Public Health, with the administrative and coordination tasks fulfilled by the National Board of Health and Welfare. The National Board of Health and Welfare is in charge of the supervision of medical care and social services, of follow-up studies and official statistics. Additionally, the National Institute of Public Health fulfils coordination tasks and stimulates high scientific standards. In Public Health, cooperation is a major characteristic of the policy-making, which is needed for the successful policy outcome. For the planning and construction of major infrastructure projects, a consultative committee of the Ministry of Trade and Industry has been set up. However, the major transport infrastructure is still planned, decided and implemented in a rather conventional and centralised way. Nevertheless, the local authorities have recently made increasing use of informal channels of access and lobbying structures. This tendency has led to a trend of a bottom-up rethinking of the policy-making and increasing municipal initiatives in the policy field. In Regional and Structural Policy, formal consultative procedures have diminished over time and have been replaced by informal hearings and information meetings. Additionally, regional growth agreements have been concluded, which use the increasing value of European dimension of Regional Policy. On the informal level of cooperation and coordination, a significant influence of the social partners can be identified for the ESF programmes, with the programmes being worked out in partnership with the social partners.

5. *Two-Tiered States*

5.1 Greece

General Forms of Cooperation

The sub-national level is consulted on General Training aspects within a general form of cooperation and coordination that takes place in the two-tiered system of Greece. The Prefect, which operates as state representative in the regions, acts as further coordinating body for all policy fields.

Formalised cooperation is taken place to a lesser extent between the levels of government, but on the national level with the specialised agencies.

Policy Field Specific Characteristics

In General Training Policy, the national ministries of Education and Labour cooperate in the policy formulation. Furthermore, a significant role has the Organisation of Development of the Workforce (OAED), which is an administratively autonomous body acting under the supervision of the national Ministry of Employment and Social Security. Within the Youth Policy, the General Secretariat for Youth (GGNO), which operates within the national Ministry of Education, is in charge of the formulation and coordination of government policy on Youth. On the local level, Youth Policy does not have significant importance and there is no tradition of local Youth Policy in Greece. For the formulation and implementation of Culture, numerous special regional bodies operate under the supervision of the Ministry, such as various museums and other cultural institutions. A further example of formulised cooperation within the policy field of Culture is the National Cultural Network of the Cities (NCNC). Currently, there is only very limited need and actual practice of cooperation and coordination in Public Health between the different levels in Greece. The same is true for the informal forms of influence of the sub-national level in the public health sector. On the sub-national level, 17 secretary generals for Public Health are nominated by the central government, which are located on the local level, but depend on the central government. The current balance of power between the central and the sub-national level might change in the near future with the planned regional health systems and the aim of the national government to restructure the service provision by giving the regions a greater share in the policy implementation. For the transport infrastructure planning within the national system, the local level is consulted on major infrastructure projects and the participation in the EU programmes. The Regional and Structural Policy can be characterised as central field of the decentralisation process in Greece. The implementation of the EU Regional policy was a driving force in the process of decentralisation in Greece. After this decentralisation has taken place, the selection of funded projects from the Cohesion fund is made after a suggestion from the Regional Council, special observer committees. When evaluating the overall political role of the regions in the implementation, the role of the regions and the regional autonomy is still rather limited. Centralisation can be observed in the administration of the European Social Fund.

5.2 Ireland

General Forms of Cooperation

The sub-national level takes part in the policy process within the bi-cameral parliament, which serves as a general form of coordination and consultation between the different levels. The bi-cameral parliament serves as a general, institutionalised channel of access for the sub-national authorities and as a form of cooperation between the different levels.

Policy Field Specific Characteristics

In the policy field of General Training, the central, coordinating training body is the Training and Employment Authority (Foras Áiseanna Saothair, FAS). FAS is based in Dublin, but runs various centres throughout the country. It also coordinates and directs the state monopoly in vocational training and other training policy areas. For the area of Youth Policy, the National Youth Council, also based in Dublin, fulfils important coordination tasks in close cooperation with FAS. The National Youth Council has had a monopoly in the formulation of Youth Policy but the public authorities started a programme of privatisation in the 1990s. Voluntary associations at local, regional and national level, local youth associations have a strong influence on policy making. In the area of informal cooperation and de facto political influence it can be observed that it has traditionally been difficult for the local bodies to gain state or indeed European accreditation or funding for training initiatives. With respect to the informal, political perspective, it is furthermore important to point to the interrelation of EU integration, the work of the CoR and the domestic regional development. These aspects have been interrelated, reinforcing trends in the political debate. With respect to political practice and the forms of cooperation in the policy field of Culture, a continuing process of devolution of powers and responsibilities can be observed. In Public Health, formalised forms of cooperation are taking place between central government and the local agencies (health boards), which provide the service. When analysing political practice in this policy field, it is obvious that the national agencies still play a dominant, influential role in the formulation and implementation of Health Policy. The support framework of the European Social Fund has been instrumental in bringing third level training and education to a new generation of school-leavers, both with respect to grants and funding.

A further aspect of the political practice in the area of the ESF is the fact that a growing number of local interest groups are seeking direct dialogue with Brussels, while bypassing national organs and political channels. ERDF cooperation primarily operates through partnership provided for the EU programmes and involve local players. Furthermore, local authorities try to use informal channels and direct contacts in Brussels to influence the policy-making process.

5.3 Luxembourg

General Forms of Cooperation

The national and local authorities cooperate closely on policy-making.

Policy Field Specific Characteristics

The Youth Policy in Luxembourg, for example, is coordinated between the Ministry of Family, Social Solidarity and Youth and the municipalities. The National Youth Authority fulfils a further, coordinating function. For Transeuropean Networks and major infrastructure projects, cooperation between the national level and the municipalities takes place for the elaboration of an interregional concept of transport and infrastructure policy. Similar coordination takes place for Regional and Structural Policy between the Ministry of Economy and the municipalities in the eligible areas.

IV. National Surveys on the Distribution of Tasks within the fields of Mandatory Consultation

1. General Training and Youth

Until the Treaty of Maastricht, EC activities in the training sector where mainly concentrated on vocational training. The Community had only very limited competencies in the policy area of General Training, which were based on other legal norms. The Treaty on the European Union introduced General Training and Youth as own chapter in the TEC. The separate legal basis served as basis for the clarification of the scope and framework for community policies and activities. In its legal, institutional and procedural structure, the regulation of EU activities in General Training (art. 149 EC (ex-art. 126)) and Vocational Training (art. 150 EC (ex-art. 127)) are similar. However, the scope for community action in vocational training is considerably wider compared to the policy field of General Training.

The main objective of General Training and Youth is to develop quality education in the Member States at pre-school, school and university level. To ensure this, the EU supports and completes in a complementary manner the policies of the Member States. Within the framework of this overall orientation, three main objectives can be identified: The development of a European Dimension of General Training, the support of mobility and the encouragement of international cooperation in General Training and Youth Policy. The policy includes: promoting of teaching and dissemination of European languages, encouraging mobility of students and teachers, promoting cooperation between educational establishments, developing exchanges of information and experience on education issues, encouraging youth exchanges and exchange of socio-educational instructors, and encouraging the development of distance education. The term "training" used in the context of the EU General Training Policy is to be understood in an inclusive way, covering state owned, private, institutionalised and ad-hoc training.

In order to implement the objectives of art. 149 EC (ex-art. 126) the EU adopts incentive measures in form of programmes. Currently there are three major programmes in the field of education and youth: Socrates (school education, higher and adult education, language, and distance learning), Youth (Youth exchanges, European Voluntary Service, and Youth initiatives), and Tempus III (curricular development and structural reform of higher education in cooperation with countries of Central and Eastern Europe). Leonardo is not a part of the policy field General Training and Youth, since it deals with vocational training issues. Youth Policy in the EU context is integrated in the overall policy framework of General Training Policy and equally regulated in art. 149 EC (ex-art. 126).

Academic recognition of diplomas is specified as an objective of art. 149 EC (ex-art. 126). However, decisions in this area are mainly made according to art. 47 EC (ex-art. 57), which does not provide for CoR consultation. Therefore, academic recognition of diplomas will not be dealt with in this study.

In General Training and Youth Policy, the EU fulfils the function of coordination and support. The policy concentrates more on a catalytic and complementary function, than on setting up own, EU specific policy objectives. In General Training and Youth, the EU uses mainly the instruments of support programmes and recommendations.

General Training and Youth Policy on the EU level is closely interrelated and interconnected with a large number of other EU policies. Giving a comprehensive overview on these forms of intersections and interrelations would be beyond the scope and purpose of this study. However, the main forms of coordination shall be mentioned. Beside the general competency for General and Vocational Training, for which the TEC foresees mandatory consultation rights for the CoR according to article 149 EC (ex-art. 126) and 150 EC (ex-art. 127), training measures are also covered by article 164 lit d as far as the mobility of researchers and the EU research and technology policy is concerned. Similar interrelations can be observed for training measures in the context of the Common Agricultural Policy and the policies covered by the ECSC treaty. A close, institutionalised and legally foreseen interrelation has furthermore been established between the community policy on General Training and Vocational Training and the European Social Fund, with EU programmes in this area being financed by the ESF. Additionally, training measures form an important part of the European Social Policy as regulated in article 137 2. EC (ex-art. 118 A 2.).

Beside these forms of interrelation and intersection with other, specific EU policies, General Training is also closely interconnected with the implementation of the basic freedoms. In this context, it should be emphasized that the EU General Training Policy aims at reducing existing limitations to the free movement of labour resulting from national training measures. It should be noted in this context that, analysing the policy output, the measures based on article 149 EC (ex-art. 126) and those based on article 47 2. EC (ex-art. 57 2.) are very closely interrelated. Recognition of diplomas is, however, strictly based on article 47 2. EC (ex-art. 57 2.), which does not provide for the CoR mandatory consultation. Beside the interrelation with the basic freedom of free movement for workers, General Training Policy also affects the freedom of services, for example in the case of training institutions, which seek to provide their services also in other EU Member States. The interrelation between the basic freedoms and the EU General Training policy covers furthermore the access to public and private training institutions and financial support for training. As for other policy fields, the principle of non-discrimination (article 12 EC (ex-art. 6)) applies also to the policy field of General Training and Youth. The Youth Policy measures and programmes on the EU level are closely related both to General Training and Vocational Training.

Within the policy field of General Training and Youth, it is furthermore of vital importance to emphasize the application of the principle of subsidiarity and additionality. Member States have sole responsibility for curricula and the educational system. According to art. 149 4. EC (ex-art. 126 4.) any harmonization of legal and administrative regulations is forbidden. These provisions are an expression of the subsidiarity principle as laid down in art. 5 EC (ex-art. 3 b). This limitation of community actions has been designed to protect and safeguard the sphere of competencies of the Member States and regions. Activities of the EU are furthermore limited by their function, as being supportive and complementary. The EU programmes correspond to the thematically determined, national general training policies. The national policy serves as basis of orientation and focal point for the development of EU policies. As general principle and guiding norm for EU activities in the sphere of article 149 EC (ex-art. 126), the principle of subsidiarity applies. The principle of subsidiarity implies that the specific EU actions in the field of General Training cannot be managed sufficiently on the national or regional level and that these objectives can be reached in a better way on the EU level.

When analysing the understanding of the policy field of General Training and Youth in the 15 Member States it is important to emphasize that the political agenda of the policy field in the national context is much broader and more controversial. The policy field of General Training covers all aspects of education in the Member States, including a structured educational system and the determination of the content and curricula of education. The EU programmes for General Training and Youth form an integral part and are closely inte connected with the aims and objectives of the national general training policy in order to give a comprehensive overview on the policy field of General Training and Youth, the research team agreed to expand the surveys beyond those areas, which are covered by Community action. Therefore, the surveys will include the main elements of the structure and organisation of the general training systems as well as the content and dimensions of General Training Policy in the Member States. In the following tables on the Member States, "educational policy" and "General Training are used synonymously for the same policy field.

Youth Policy in the national context is treated either as a separate policy in a large number of Member States (e.g. Germany, Austria, France and others), or as a cross-cutting policy, which is closely interrelated with a large number of other policy fields, especially education, employment, culture and social policy. At EU level, Youth Policy is integrated into the overall General Training Policy, is regulated in the same article (article 149 EC) and focuses on youth exchange. This interrelation and integration of Youth Policy and General Training is significantly closer than in most Member States. As for General Training, the political agenda for Youth Policy in the EU Member States is much broader. Furthermore, certain, specific national characteristics have to be taken into consideration when analysing the understanding of General Training and Youth Policy in the 15 Member States as for example the strong influence of consociational principles in certain Member States.

Turning from the differences in the understanding to the distribution of competencies the analysis of the 15 Member States clearly indicates that General Training belongs to a major competency of the sub-national level in federal and regionalised states, however, with certain exceptions (e.g. in the case of Austria). The general rules and standards are fixed in all categories of states by the national level, which indicates a strong need for cooperation and joint policy-making in all those states, where the sub-national level takes a significant share in General Training Policy. Shared competencies and policy responsibility are a typical characteristic of General Training Policy in most EU Member States. In the implementation of this shared responsibility a close network of institutionalised and informal cooperation and consultation has been established between the different levels of government. However, it has to be mentioned that the scope for action with regard to the sub-national level is considerably lower for decentralised and two-tiered states, compared to federal and regionalised states.

1.1 Federal States

1.1.1 Austria

Characteristics	Federal Government	Regional Government - Länder	Local Government
General Training Policy Nine year compulsory school Structured school system, 4 years of primary school, 4 years secondary modern school (*"Hauptschule"*) plus poly-technical education, furthermore grammar school of 8 years Non-compulsory pre-school education School systems levels are comparatively flexible Additional system of poly-technical education (more explicit focus on the preparation for vocational training) Providing and maintaining high quality of education based on knowledge transfer, the needs of the information society General principle of free access to education Principle of life-long-learning	*General Training Policy* Setting of legislative framework for General Training General principles, system's levels and curricula regulated in the law on schools (*"Schulgesetzwerk"*) General Training Policy implementation with respect to the organisation of the school system, the internal organisation of the educational system, large sector of policy implementation by own organs (*"unmittelbare Bundesverwaltung"*)	*General Training Policy* Participation in the implementation of General Training Policy within the framework set by the federal level Legislation on and implementation of pre-school education Limited margin of the Länder for setting own priorities, limited scope for action of the Länder in the context of the policy implementation, e.g. in the context of the regulation of curricula, public subsidies in the field of education etc.	*General Training Policy* Shared responsibility with the Länder for personal of preschool education Setting-up and running of facilities of primary and secondary modern schools Responsibility for polytechnical education (*"Polytechnische*

Characteristics	Federal Government	Regional Government - Länder	Local Government
Almost uniform regulation of General Training Policy in Austria Cleavages not along territorial, but ideological / confessional lines Public school system free of charge, university education not free of charge (since 2001)	Universities owned by the state, school system regulated on federal level Legislation on the status of teachers in public schools		*Lehrgänge*")
Youth Policy Youth Policy includes wide range of activities (youth programmes and youth exchange, important role of youth associations in shaping of Youth Policy	*Youth Policy* Limited competencies of the federal level in Youth Policy by providing a legal framework and general policy guidelines in certain areas of youth policy	*Youth Policy* Youth policy falls under Länder responsibility, focus on providing support for and cooperating with free associations ("*freie Träger*")	*Youth Policy* Participation in the implementation of Youth Policy projects and programmes

1.1.2 Belgium

Characteristics	Federal Government	Regional Government		Local Government
		Regions	Communities	Provinces / Municipalities
General Training Policy	*General Training Policy*	----	*General Training Policy*	*General Training Policy*
General Training and Youth rather separate policy fields, link between General Training and Vocational Training	Only limited, basic principles regulated on Federal level		General Training major part of their competency	Provinces and Municipalities take initiatives within their general competency for regulating local affairs
Pre-school education part of cultural affairs	Federal government sets beginning and end of compulsory education		Competency applies to linguistically defined areas	Participation in the policy implementation according to the rules and norms set by the federal level and the Communities
Specific importance of providing skills for professional life	Regulation of minimum conditions for diploma		Competency includes general guidelines, financing, school transport, and grants for students etc.	
Implementation of the principle of equal opportunities				Provinces and municipalities bear responsibilities in the field of education, as for example the running of general training infrastructure
Parallel structure of public and private schools, freedom of choice, both forms receive state funding from the community level, education is free of charge	Determines syndical status and pension schemes for teachers			50 % of provincial expenditure is related to General Training Policy
School education is structured in various levels and forms, 6 years of primary education, compulsory				28 % of municipal expenditure

Characteristics	Federal Government	Regional Government		Local Government
		Regions	Communities	Provinces / Municipalities
education lasts from the age of 6 to 15-16 years of age, education structured in general course, technical course, additional seventh year leads to highest school leaving exam Higher education in universities either church affiliated or free, university education lasts approximately four years				is related to General Training Policy
Youth Policy Youth policy corresponds to needs of young people, support development of the personality of youth, policy linked to other policies (e.g. employment)	---	---	*Youth Policy* Youth policy formulation and implementation Legal framework for Youth Policy	---

1.1.3 Germany

Characteristics	Federal Government	Regional Government – Länder	Local Government
General Training Policy	*General Training Policy*	*General Training Policy*	*General Training Policy*
Organisation of pre-school, school and higher education and vocational training	Since the 1970s (constitutional amendment): framework competency for legislation and policies to support scientific research and education ("*Ausbildungsförderung*")	General Training major competency of the Länder	General competency for regulating local affairs, local self-administration according to art. 28 BL
Policy-shaping and content of General Training Policy varies between the Länder	Joint policy making of the Federal level and the Länder in certain fields of General Training ("*Gemeinschaftsaufgabe*"), as the construction of universities and the support of research programmes	Länder determine curricula of education (General Training and higher education, cooperation between the Länder for setting minimum conditions of diploma	Responsibility for pre-school education
School education: four years of primary school, 5 years of secondary modern school ("*Hauptschule*") or 6 years of secondary modern school ("*Realschule*"), grammar school of 9 years	Regulation on the access to universities for foreigners	Content of General Training policy varies between the Länder	Responsibility for running primary schools (facilities, educational infrastructure etc.)
General Training free of charge, public school financed by the Länder		Norms on information exchange between institutions of education	
Comparatively small sector of private schools and general training institutions		Participation in programmes for the mobility of	
Higher education. Constitutional guarantee of freedom of science, structured system of forms and degree of higher education			
Large part of General Training are attributed to the sphere of cultural affairs			

Characteristics	Federal Government	Regional Government – Länder	Local Government
("*Kulturhoheit*") as a major competency of the Länder		students	
Youth Policy Youth Policy treated rather separately from General Training, important role of private associations ("*freie Träger*") Central objective is to provide a contribution to the development of skills and personality of young people	*Youth Policy* Limited competencies in Youth policy: Legislation on aid for children and youth, covering social and fiscal aspects of Youth Policy ("*Kinder- & Jugendhilfegesetz*)	*Youth Policy* Youth policy formulation and setting up of youth policy programmes Support of Youth associations Several Länder run own Youth programmes	*Youth Policy* Provide framework for Youth associations and independent associations active in Youth Policy Implementation of Youth policy

1.2 Regionalised States

1.2.1 France

Characteristics	National Government	Regional Authorities – Régions	Local Authorities – Départements / Communes
General Training Policy	*General Training Policy*	*General Training Policy*	*General Training Policy*
Provision of education needed for professional life	Providing of legislative framework for General Training	School administration organised on the regional level, supervisory power on certain educational institutions (for example lycées)	Communes are in charge of providing primary schools
Interdependence of general education, professional education and Youth Policy	Sets the general objectives and policy orientation		Départements are competent for establishing collèges
Close link between General Training and Employment Policy	Construction and maintenance of universities		Administrative school planning (definition of general needs, identifying need for investment, running facilities, except for universities)
Public school and university system, policy-shaping in General Training Policy dominated by the national government	Personnel recruitment, instruction of teachers, general personnel planning		
At all levels of education, private institutions of General Training have been established parallel to the public system, private schools under state supervision	Setting up and running of facilities for universities		
Compulsory school covers primary and secondary education and lasts up to the age of 16 years, structured school system	Content and curricula for General Training decided on the national level		

Characteristics	National Government	Regional Authorities – Régions	Local Authorities – Départements / Communes
Non-compulsory pre-school education, pre-school education much more used than in other European states University education: very differentiated and complex system, various types of higher education *Youth Policy* In Youth Policy, the main priority is setting the legal and organisational framework for private associations active in the sector Further sectors of the French Youth Policy cover the international youth exchange, General Training and education for youth, youth employment programmes, youth information and the support of youth activities	*Youth Policy* Legislation on youth affairs, control of legal norms related to youth policy Responsibility for setting policy guidelines and framework for youth education, youth employment, youth information and communication and youth exchange National government also active in promoting and supporting youth activities	---	*Youth Policy* Policy implementation according to the nationally set objectives and in the context of the national youth programmes Implementation of youth activities, youth education measures and other policies in cooperation with the private youth associations Support of youth initiatives and youth association on the local level

1.2.2 Italy

Characteristics	National Government	Regional Authorities – Regions	Local Authorities	
			Provinces	Municipalities
General Training Policy Provision of adequate education for young people School system is structured in pre-school education, primary school, secondary modern school (two levels) and grammar schools 10 years of compulsory school education Fairly unitarian practice of General Training Policy General Training based on traditional, knowledge-based education and practical humanistic culture Dividing line between theoretical, knowledge-based education and practical education (professional education and vocational training) Uniform school leaving exams in the whole country	*General Training Policy* General principles for General Training Policy Providing legal and political framework of General Training	*General Training Policy* Competency for professional education and school assistance Regions are bound by general principles laid down by the national legislation Administrative tasks in General Training Responsibility for school assistance (guaranteeing equal opportunities), administration of state and own funds for school assistance	*General Training Policy* All policy implementation tasks, for which there is no need for uniform implementation, are transferred from the regions to the local level, overlapping competencies with municipalities Participation in General Training Policy in the context of local self administration Several provinces	*General Training Policy* All policy implementation tasks, for which there is no need for uniform implementation, are transferred from the regions to the local level, overlapping competencies with provinces Participation in General Training Policy in the context of local self administration

Characteristics	National Government	Regional Authorities – Regions	Local Authorities	
			Provinces	Municipalities
University education: large variety of subjects and degrees Parallel structure of public and private universities, large variety in fees			have set up institutes of higher education, specific focus and priority on General Training projects and policies in several provinces	20% of municipal expenditure related to General Training

The constitutional reform of March 2001 has transferred further responsibilities of General Training Policy to the regions in a rather general manner, differentiating between general norms of education on the one hand, which are reserved for the national government and the principle of autonomy in education, which belongs to the concurrent legislative power (art. 117 of the Constitution). This reform proposal was subject to a referendum in October 2001 and has been approved by 64.2 % of the voters. Therefore, the political consequences of this current reform process remain to be seen.

Characteristics	National Government	Regional Authorities – Regions	Local Authorities	
			Provinces	Municipalities
Youth Policy	*Youth Policy*	*Youth Policy*	*Youth Policy*	*Youth Policy*
Youth policy not separate policy field, but integrated into various policy fields (social policy, employment policy)	National, coordinating role in youth policy is rather weak	Development and implementation of youth policy programmes	Development and implementation of youth policy programmes	Development and implementation of youth policy programmes
Certain focus on youth exchange	Youth exchange is allocated within a special office in the Ministry of Foreign Affairs, which has set up regional branches			

1.2.3 Portugal

Characteristics	National Government	Regional Authorities		Local Authorities	
		Autonomous regions	Districts / Regional Boards of National Ministries	Municipalities	Parishes
General Training Policy	*General Training Policy*	*General Training Policy*		*General Training Policy*	*General Training Policy*
Organisation of structured school system and higher education	Policy guidelines, legislative framework and policy objectives set by the national level	General Training and Youth policy formulation and implementation lies within the competency of the regional governments of the autonomous regions		Limited role and competencies of the local level	Participation in the municipal policy making via programming contracts
Voluntary pre-school education	Supervision of policy implementation	Regional governments adapt the general policy objectives set by the national government to the local context		Providing of facilities for primary education	Activities in the context of the maintenance of school buildings
Dual structure of private and public schools	Determination of content and curricula of education				
Compulsory school from the age of 6 to 16, further, secondary school education		For continental Portugal, the policy of General Training is formulated by the national government and implemented by the Districts / Regional Boards of National Ministers, partly in cooperation with the local authorities			
Dual structure of public and church-affiliated schools					

Characteristics	National Government	Regional Authorities		Local Authorities	
		Autonomous regions	Districts / Regional Boards of National Ministries	Municipalities	Parishes
Youth Policy High priority for Youth Policy Integrated approach coordinated with other policies	*Youth Policy* Policy guidelines and objective for youth policy Development of youth policy programmes and activities	*Youth Policy* Youth policy formulation and implementation lies within the competency of the regional governments of the autonomous regions. Regional governments adapt the general policy objectives set by the national government to the local context For continental Portugal, the policy formulation and implementation remains with the districts / regional boards of the national ministry, which cooperate with the local authorities		*Youth Policy* Participation in youth policy implementation Youth policy initiatives on voluntary basis	*Youth Policy* Participation in the municipal policy making via programming contracts

1.2.4 Spain

Characteristics	National Government	Regional Authorities – Autonomous Communities (AC)	Local Authorities – Provinces and Municipalities
General Training Policy	*General Training Policy*	*General Training Policy*	*General Training Policy*
Improvement of the quality of teaching and religious instruction	Providing legislative framework, supervisory power on policy implementation	General Training policy implementation and administration for the ACs with higher political status, regulating power and management competency for specific areas of General Training (Andalusia, Canary Islands, Catalonia, Galicia, Basque Country, Navarra, Valencia)	Pre-school education and elementary schools organised on local level
Close link between General Training and Vocational Training Policy	Organisation of system's levels, requirements for diploma, basic rules for General Training		Competency for organising complementary activities of the institutions of lower education (seminars, workshops, artistic and sport activities etc.)
Inclusion of youth into professional life			
Parallel structure of public and private schools, private sector comparatively small	Concurrent legislative power for scientific and technical research (both national level and AC's are active)	For the other ACs General Training remains competency of the national level	Overall limited competencies of the local level in General Training
Constitutional right to respect religion in General Training Policy			
Constitutional Norm of freedom of science	Both national level and Autonomous Communities have own competency for setting up universities	Concurrent legislative power for scientific and technical research (both
Compulsory school of 10 years			
Voluntary pre-school education			
University education lasts approximately 3 to 5 years, universities are attributed the right of self-administration			
Fees at universities are comparatively high			

Characteristics	National Government	Regional Authorities – Autonomous Communities (AC)	Local Authorities – Provinces and Municipalities
Primary and secondary modern school free of charge		technical research (both national level and ACs are active) Both national level and Autonomous Communities own competency for setting up universities	
Youth Policy Youth: providing framework for youth to take part in political, social and cultural activities Close link of youth policy to other policies as General Training, employment etc. Support personal development of young people, education, cultural activities, support of youth associations, youth health, youth information	*Youth Policy* Setting of policy guidelines and legal framework Coordinating function Youth institute set up by Ministry of Social Affairs	*Youth Policy* ACs are in charge of various specific aspects of Youth Policy (e.g. youth education)	*Youth Policy* Implementation of Youth Policy programmes Development of large scale of youth policy activities Running of youth policy infrastructure (youth centres)

1.2.5 United Kingdom

Characteristics	Central Government	Regional Authorities	Local Authorities
General Training Policy Professional training and higher education covered by General Training Policy Principle of life-long learning Classical, humanistic model of education for higher education and vocational training Structured school system, various levels of school education, 9 year compulsory school Parallel structure of private and public schools, both public and private financing of general training services Pre-school education provided as part time child-care	*General Training Policy* National government sets policy framework and general legal norms Policy guidelines and coordination by Department for Education and Employment	*General Training Policy* *Scottish Parliament:* Legislative and executive power on General Training, including schools and higher education within the framework set by the central government Scottish executive administers policy on school and pre-school education within the framework set by the central government *National Assembly for Wales:* Responsibility for General Training and Youth has been transferred to Wales within the framework set by the central government (secondary legislative power) *Northern Ireland Assembly:* Competency for General Training and Youth at regional level within	*General Training Policy* Local activities deriving from its governing legislation (statutes) County Councils bear responsibilities in the field of education: local level runs almost all schools, including specialised schools for handicapped people, local level administers educational system School administration on the local level: responsibility for school buildings, staff employment and teaching material

Characteristics	Central Government	Regional Authorities	Local Authorities
		the framework set by the central government	
		English Regional Development Agencies (RDAs)	
		Annual report on General Training and Youth	
		RDAs contribute to General Training programmes and policies	
		Government Offices for the Regions (GOR)	
		Support education and training in England	
		Coordination and participation in policy implementation in England	
Youth Policy	*Youth Policy*	*Youth Policy*	*Youth Policy*
Youth Policy integrated in other, sectorial policies (employment, education etc.) Youth policy guided by educational aspects, aim to promote equal opportunities	Limited role in Youth Policy formulation by providing the legal framework for certain areas closely related to Youth Policy (rights of children etc.)	Youth policy has been devolved to the regional governments of England, Scotland, Wales and Northern Ireland (National Youth Agency, Youth Agency in Wales, Scottish Youth Agency, Youth Council in Northern Ireland)	Participation in the implementation of Youth Policy programmes based on statutes and governmental legislation

1.3 Decentralised States

1.3.1 Denmark

Characteristics	National Government	Regional Level (counties – "amter")	Local Level (municipalities – "kommuner")
General Training Policy Focus on life-long-learning Organisation of school forms and higher education (nine-year compulsory school, regulation of non-compulsory education) Close link to vocational training Similar approach as in EU context General right to free education since 1814, right of free education does not establish a constraint (no prohibition of private institutions) Compulsory school of 9 years, additional, structured school system, highest degree after 12 years Public and private schools, about 10% of	*General Training Policy* Providing legislative framework, supervision of different branches of education (Ministry of Education) Overall defining power for General Training Policy Policy covers pre-school, school and higher education	*General Training Policy* A number of specific tasks in General Training policy have been assigned to the counties, as for example the management of grammar schools	*General Training Policy* Supervision and administration of primary schools and secondary schools under the overall supervision of the national ministry

Characteristics	National Government	Regional Level (counties – "amter")	Local Level (municipalities – "kommuner")
a particular year attend private schools			
Highly structured school system			
Structured higher / university education providing for short cycle, medium-cycle and long-cycle higher education			
Public financing of education, based on grants related to the level of pupil/student activity, measured in full-time semesters or years			
Higher, university education lasts approximately 5 years			
Youth Policy	*Youth Policy*	*Youth Policy*	*Youth Policy*
No specific, separate Youth Policy, Youth policy integrated in social and leisure time activities	Legal framework for Youth Policy provided by national level	The counties are not involved in the genuine Youth Policy within the national system.	Youth Policy implementation and administration, integrated into social policy
	Definition of policy guidelines and overall policy framework for Youth Policy measures	However, regional competencies in other policy fields might be affected in the implementation of Youth Policy. Youth Policy objectives might, for example, be	

Characteristics	National Government	Regional Level (counties – "amter")	Local Level (municipalities – "kommuner")
		affected in the management of grammar schools	

1.3.2 Finland

Characteristics	National Government	Regional Level - Provinces	Local Level
General Training Policy Broad understanding of General Training Policy Constitutional right of education, equal opportunities, education free of charge (public financing of education) Freedom of arts, science and higher education Structured educational system (pre-school, education, structured school system and higher education) 9 years of compulsory school Universities are state owned and provide for lower (B.A.), higher (M.A.) and postgraduate degrees, universities are run by the state, government provides 70% of their funding Polytechnics in municipal or private ownership	*General Training Policy* Legal framework for General Training Policy Setting of main policy objectives and guidelines for General Training Policy Definition of degrees and content of university education Regulation of standards for curricula and content of education in accordance with the principle of life-long learning	*General Training Policy* Administration and policy implementation in cooperation with local authorities Important function of the provinces in the policy implementation	*General Training Policy* Central role in policy making and policy implementation Service providing function Responsibility for comprehensive schools and educational institutions (service providing function)
Youth Policy Youth policy closely related to General Training, similar approach Focus on youth education, youth employment, youth workshops	*Youth Policy* Legislation on policy guidelines for Youth Policy	*Youth Policy* Limited participation in the Youth Policy in the context of the general supervision and	*Youth Policy* Local level particular active in implementing youth policy programmes

Characteristics	National Government	Regional Level - Provinces	Local Level
workshops		administrative control of the municipalities, they fulfil a number of specific administrative tasks	

1.3.3 The Netherlands

Characteristics	National Government	Regional Level – Provinces	Local Level – Municipalities
General Training Policy	*General Training Policy*	*General Training Policy*	*General Training Policy*
Close interrelation of General Training and the principle of consociational democracy	Governmental policy limited to public schools, principle of non-intervention to church-based education (separate, church-affiliated school administration)	Provincial activities in the area of General Training limited to public schools	Municipal policy limited to public schools
Freedom of Education crucial factor in the political tension of the 19th and early 20th century		Limited influence on policy shaping due to sensitivity of the policy field	Limited influence on policy shaping due to sensitivity of the policy field
Parallel structure of public and denomination-based (church-affiliated) schools, both sectors state financed	Predominant level for policy formulation and setting policy guidelines (Ministry of Education)	Provinces take part in policy implementation (service providing function for the public sector of General Training Policy)	Municipalities take part in policy implementation (service providing function for the public sector of General Training Policy)
General Training policy covers all forms of education from pre-school to university	Determination of policy guidelines and legal framework for higher education		
Government prescribes general terms of education (subjects) and graduation levels			
Integrated pre-school and primary school starting at the age of 4, compulsory school lasts until the age of 16, further			

Characteristics	National Government	Regional Level – Provinces	Local Level – Municipalities
education split in vocational sector and upper secondary and grammar school sector			
Youth Policy Support of children and young people in their development Child day care and preventive youth policy	*Youth Policy* National government (Ministry for Well-being, Health and Sport) sets policy guidelines of Youth policy Legal framework provided by national level	*Youth Policy* Implementation of Youth policy programmes, level of responsibility (provinces or municipalities) varies according to programme	*Youth Policy* Implementation of Youth policy programmes, level of responsibility (provinces or municipalities) varies according to programme

1.3.4 Sweden

Characteristics	National Government	Regional Level (counties – "län" / county councils "landsting")	Local Level (municipalities – "kommuner")
General Training Policy Broad understanding of General Training Policy, covering all aspects of education (pre-school to universities) Principle of integrated learning and personal development Pre-school is part of the obligatory school, structured school system with various degrees, 9 years of compulsory school School education free of charge (financial resources provided by the public authorities) Ongoing discussion on and use of alternative pedagogy Rising private sector for school education	*General Training Policy* Policy formulation and provision of legal framework by national government and parliament Responsibility for policy formulation at different levels of education (pre-school, school, universities) National Board for Education is in charge of detailed regulation (curricula, supervision of schools)	*General Training Policy* Counties are responsible for running people's high-schools (preparatory institutions for upper secondary or university studies) Counties are in charge of the nursery-schools (closely linked to the counties responsibility in public health)	*General Training Policy* Responsibility for policy implementation Local school plans are adapted to the given objectives Management of upper secondary school system, often on an inter-municipal basis Running of schools and universities Employers for school staff and teachers

Characteristics	National Government	Regional Level (counties – "län" / county councils "landsting")	Local Level (municipalities – "kommuner")
National Agency for Education with supervisory functions Higher education: universities are owned by the state, they have large freedom in organisation matters *Youth Policy* Youth policy in weak position Proactive Youth policy rather weak phenomenon Application of the best-practice approach in Youth Policy Active role of private associations	*Youth Policy* Policy formulation and provision of legal framework National level closely cooperates with local authorities in Youth Policy State agency "National Board of Youth": coordinating function, stimulates research and know-how related to the youth policy objectives	*Youth Policy* Limited competency of the counties in Youth Policy if and as far as Youth Policy matters are related to public health and medical care	*Youth Policy* Policy implementation within the framework of the nationally set policy objectives Close cooperation between the national level and the municipalities in concrete youth policy programmes and policy implementation Main responsibility for Youth Policy shaping is allocated on local level

1.4 Two-Tiered States

1.4.1 Greece

Characteristics	National Government	Intermediary Institutions I - Regions	Intermediary Institutions II - Prefectures	Local Authorities – Municipalities
General Training Policy Broad understanding, covering all aspects of education Personal development at all levels of education (pre-school, school, vocational training, universities) Differentiated, structured school system Non-compulsory pre-school education starting at the age of 3 Nine-year compulsory school 12 years school education to the highest school leaving exam (uniform exam for the whole country) High education / universities with strict admission control, recent reform proposals	*General Training Policy* Policy formulation and providing of legal framework National governments set policy guidelines and main objectives for General Training including higher / university education Specialised, national bodies have important role in policy implementation	--	--	*General Training Policy* Consultation and hearing rights in the policy formulation Policy implementation in cooperation with national government

Characteristics	National Government	Intermediary Institutions I - Regions	Intermediary Institutions II - Prefectures	Local Authorities – Municipalities
Both public and private institutions of higher education				
Youth Policy Youth Policy aims at supporting the development and capacities of young people Aim of supporting participation of youth in society Main areas: youth information, youth exchange, financial support for social, educational and leisure activities	*Youth Policy* Policy formulation and legal framework Coordinating body: Secretary General for Youth, subordinate to the Ministry of Education	---	---	*Youth Policy* Local level not very active in Youth policy Setting up of youth centres, implementation of specific youth measures No clearly defined competencies for Youth Policy

1.4.2 Ireland

Characteristics	National Government	Geographic Regions - Provinces	Local Authorities – County Councils (and local authorities grouped around counties or large cities)
General Training Policy High priority of General Training on the national level National General Training Policy linked to the aim of the reduction of unemployment Broad understanding, including education from pre-school to university level Policy linked to employment and vocational training policy Uniform primary education, post primary education consists of various levels, both private and public schools Universities provide higher education: operate as private institutions, which receive public funds, both universities and private colleges Specific focus on the promotion of the	*General Training Policy* Political responsibility for General Training Policy National Ministries have central role in policy formulation and implementation Curricula for school education determined by the national government and administration, universities enjoy considerable freedom in determining curricula, standards and degrees	---	*General Training Policy* Local level received influence on General Training Policy implementation via local partnerships Primary schools under the supervision of the local authorities, significant influence of the church on primary education Secondary schools administered and controlled by the local authorities

Characteristics	National Government	Geographic Regions - Provinces	Local Authorities – County Councils (and local authorities grouped around counties or large cities)
Irish language *Youth Policy* Youth Policy orientated towards educational objectives Aim to support social environment of youth, social learning of young people and youth information	*Youth Policy* General Principles and policy guidelines Provision of legal framework Coordinating function Advisory function of the Irish Youth Council Provision of financial support for voluntary associations	---	*Youth Policy* Provision of financial support for youth association Setting up and financing of youth programmes Interrelation of local youth policy and local activities in the area of vocational training

The provinces are traditional territorial entities within the Irish political system, which have, however, no regional power or policy responsibility within the policy field of General Training and Youth.

1.4.3 Luxembourg

Characteristics	National Government	Local Authorities – Municipalities
General Training Policy	*General Training Policy*	*General Training Policy*
Review and improvement of the quality of Education	Providing legal framework and policy formulation	Participation in policy implementation
Establishment and running of educational infrastructure and networks	Supervision of educational institutions	
11 years of compulsory education, including two years of compulsory pre-school education, 6 years of primary education, 3 years post primary education	Responsibility includes all levels of Education (pre-school to higher education)	
Further, structured school system with different higher degrees / grammar schools	Policy implementation by national administration in cooperation with municipalities	
General Training free of charge / financed by the state budget		
Youth Policy	*Youth Policy*	*Youth Policy*
Integrated Youth Policy, covering all economic and social aspects of the development of Youth	Preparing of legislation on Youth Policy, policy formulation and setting of policy guidelines	Setting up and running of youth centres
	Supervision of youth associations	
	Providing support for general youth education, leisure activities and setting up of youth centres	

113

2. Culture

European integration concentrated in its early phase on economic aspects of integration (establishment of a customs union, removal of barriers to trade, single market etc.). The common cultural heritage and tradition as factor, which supports a common European identity, was not recognized sufficiently. However, the economic integration promoted also cultural exchange between the Member States. The increase in intra-community trade and the increasing interdependence of the European Member States promoted the exchange of goods related to Culture (e.g. films, books). Furthermore, economic and judicial decisions had a significant influence on cultural matters. The European Court of Justice ruled, for example, in several cases on the trade of books, the regulation on television and broadcasting. Legal norms and political decisions in the policy field of Culture, as well as concerning libraries, artistic activities and intellectual property rights in the field of arts were based mainly on article 308 EC (ex-art. 235). These are areas, which have important implications for the policy field of Culture, both the developing of cultural activities on the EU level and for the national action in the policy field of culture. The introduction of Culture in the framework of EU policies by the Treaty on the European Union (Maastricht Treaty), has to be analysed against this background and the intention, also expressed in the preamble of the TEC, that integration in the economic sphere should be followed by political integration in other policy areas, with the aim of the implementation of an ever closer union of the European peoples. The Treaty on the European Union introduced a new title IX in the EC treaty on Culture and included culture, "the contribution to the flowering of European cultures" in the list of community objectives (art. 3 lit. q) EC).

The EU activities in the area of Culture, based on article 151 EC (ex-art. 128), which does not include the areas of science and education, has four main objectives: improved public knowledge about culture and history of the European peoples, preservation and protection of European cultural heritage, non-commercial cultural exchange, and prosperity of artistic and literary creativity (including the audiovisual sector). The EU is active in the development of cultural life, in the areas of media (film, radio, television) and librarianship, the preservation of national cultural goods, and the protection of copyrights for artistic works. The term of 'culture' is not defined in the treaty. However, an analysis of the treaty clarifies that cultural activities on the EU level have to be understood in a narrow sense, as the policy fields of science and research (art. 163 – 173 EC (ex-art. 130 F - ex-art. 130 P)) and General Training / education (art. 149 EC (ex-art. 126)) are covered by other EU norms. Main areas of EU activities in the field of Culture are therefore those, which can be characterised as Culture in a narrow sense, namely arts, literature, music, theatre, film, broadcasting, libraries, the protection of monuments and customs. On the one hand the EU concept of Culture is flexible and integrates also new and modern forms of culture, as for example the audiovisual media, on the other hand the TEC explicitly refuses any attempts of developing a common European Culture. On the basis of the common cultural heritage, cultural activities on the EU level aim at supporting the political integration within the Union (Calliess, 1999, S. 1468).

The EU's respective instruments in the field of Culture are multi-annual funding programs ("Culture 2000"), recommendations and symbolic actions (e.g. "European City of Culture", and "European Month of Culture"). The cross-sectional clause ensures that cultural objectives must be accounted for in the formulation of other EU policies. The main forms of political activity in the policy field of Culture on the EU level are the provision of financial support for cultural activities in the Member States and the agreement on common recommendations for cultural activities. The approach aims at supporting cultural cooperation between the Member States and contributing to the activities of the Member States. The provision of financial support for cultural cooperation between the Member States is bound to existing forms of cooperation, as the EU does not initiate forms of cooperation itself. Member States remain responsible for the thematic orientation of cultural cooperation, whereas the EU promotes the exchange of information and experiences. The provision of support by the EU for cultural activities in the Member States is not limited to a specific form of support. The most common form of support provided by the EU is a financial support programme.

Similar to the characterisation of General Training Policy, also Culture on the EU level is closely interrelated and interconnected with other policy fields. The, probably most significant, interrelation can be identified between Culture and the basic freedoms and competition law. When developing their national cultural policies, the Member States have to respect the basic freedoms guaranteed by the TEC and basic principles of competition law. However, public sponsoring of cultural activities and support for the protection of cultural heritage are compatible with the single market according to art. 87 3. lit. d) EC (ex-art. 92 3.d)).

Additionally, cultural aspects have to be considered in the policy formulation of other policies (according to art. 151 4. EC (ex-art. 128 4.) / cross-sectional clause). The clause implies to respect cultural aspects in the formulation and implementation of other community policies. The protection of the common cultural heritage can be identified as underlying objectives, which shall be considered in the formulation and implementation of all community policies.

Political interrelations between the policy field of Culture and other EU policies can furthermore be identified in several other policy fields, as for example the protection of cultural diversity of the Member States within the formulation and implementation of General Training Policy. Furthermore, EU activities in the field of Culture in the context of article 151 EC has to take into account the specialised norm of article 95 4. EC (ex-art. 100 A 4.), which defines the setting of the legal and policy framework on the national cultural heritage of the Member States as an area of national legislation.

Culture and cultural activities in the context of art. 151 EC (ex-art. 128) furthermore have to differentiate from article 47 EC (ex-art. 57) (recognition of diploma), art. 55 EC, 94 EC and 95 EC (ex-art. 66, ex-art. 100, ex-art. 100 A) (all on the adaptation of legal standards) as well as art. 149 EC (ex-art. 126) (General Training) and art. 150 EC (ex-art. 127) (Vocational

Training). These community policies might also affect the policy field of Culture and its objectives, but their main orientation and objectives are different. The legal basis for community action has to be chosen according to the subject to be regulated and the content of the planned measure.

Similar to General Training and Youth, Culture on the EU level has to take into account the principle of subsidiarity and is implemented in a complementary way. Cultural activities on the EU level have a supportive function, which is implemented in cooperation with national authorities. The complementary way, supportive function and the institutional procedure for the policy field of Culture are similar to the regulation of General Training and Vocational Training Policy. National activities in the policy field of culture form a precondition for EU activities. The EU, furthermore, has no direct influence on national cultural policies and is not competent for determining their orientation. Similarly, the EU subsidies are additional and complementary to national support. In the external cultural policy and international cultural cooperation, both the EU and the Member States are active and act in a complementary way. This approach is also expressed in the objective of the EU policy field of Culture described above, which as to be found, beside other objectives, in the protection and conservation of national and regional plurality of cultures and the protection of the common cultural heritage. The explicit exclusion of forms of harmonisation (art. 151 5. EC (ex-art. 128 5.)) applies, as long as measures in the policy field of Culture are based on article 151 EC. However, it as already been mentioned that certain measures in the framework of the policy field of Culture can also be based on other treaty norms. In this case, forms of harmonisation remain possible.

When comparing understanding of the policy field of Culture in the Member States, a significantly broader scope of the policy and larger variety of activities can be identified in the national context of the Member States compared to the EU level. Furthermore, EU activities in the policy field of Culture are closely related to a number of other policy fields in the 15 EU Member States, as to the media, broadcasting, to leisure activities and other policy areas. A certain focus on the provision of financial support, the setting of the legal framework and only a limited interference in the content and orientation of cultural activities could be identified in a large number of Member States. The central aspects of the EU Cultural activities are an integral part of national policies. As the understanding of term "Culture" is much broader in the national system of the Member States compared to the activities allocated on EU level, the research team decided to apply a similar approach as in the policy field of General Training and Youth by expanding the scope of the analysis slightly. The tabular overviews provide a comparative overview on the main characteristics of the policy field of Culture in the Member States, even if parts of these characteristics are not covered or affected by community actions.

With respect to the distribution of power and competencies, the external cultural policy is mainly allocated on national level (with the exception of Belgium), whereas various players from different levels of government are active in the remaining areas of the policy field of culture. Joint policy making is a typical characteristic in the policy field of culture, as many sub-national players depend on national funding for the implementation of concrete proposals and projects in the area of culture. The freedom for local and regional cultural activities, including the availability of resources, is much broader in federal states as Germany and Belgium than in the other EU Member States. In two-tiered states, a significant dominance of the national level could be identified even in cultural activities and programmes, with the local level taking a (limited) share in the implementation of cultural projects. For most regions, especially in federal, regionalised and decentralised states, the policy field of Culture belongs to a central field for regional and local action. This does, however, not necessarily imply that the regions and local authorities put a specific focus on this policy field in their activities and involvement on the EU level and in the EU context.

2.1 Federal States

2.1.1 Austria

Characteristics	Federal Government	Regional Government - Länder	Local Government
Broad understanding of culture	Maintenance and administration of cultural heritage (including e.g. libraries, historical monuments)	Providing support for cultural activities	Provide subsidies for cultural activities within their competency for regulating local affairs
Share in the total expenditure of the federal level and the Länder of 1.3%	Support of folk culture ("*Volkskultur*")	Set up arts competition, provide awards and scholarships, support events	Local authorities act as financier of cultural institutions (museums, orchestras)
Aim of promoting contemporary art	Providing financial support for cultural activities of the Länder and local authorities	Support cultural life by the acquisition and exhibition of arts	Parallel structure of support frameworks on the local and regional level, lack of coordination
Support of training programmes and measures for artists	Federal museums and national library	Regional activities in the policy field of Culture includes all sectors of arts	Large freedom in cultural sponsorship
Support cultural cooperation	Legislative framework for public libraries	Annual report on cultural sponsorship, further cultural publication	
Support of archives, museums, monuments and other cultural institutions	International cultural cooperation, external cultural policy and EU activities in the policy field of Culture	Parallel structure of support frameworks on the local and regional level, lack of coordination	
External cultural policy			
Various dimensions of cultural activities: folk culture ("*Volkskultur*"), elite culture etc.			
Cultural activities mainly implemented by private players			

Characteristics	Federal Government	Regional Government - Länder	Local Government
acting with public financial contribution		Important role of the Länder in the area of training, museums, archive, science and large cultural role	

2.1.2 Belgium

Characteristics	Federal Government	Regional Government		Local Government
		Regions	Communities	Provinces / Municipalities
Broad understanding of Culture, including protection of language, training, fine arts, museums and cultural institutions, libraries, discos, radio and TV, cultural aspects of youth policy, sports, leisure activities etc. Main political practice and most of the activities limited to Culture in a narrow sense (fine arts, museums, orchestras, theatres etc.) Integrated approach to the policy field of Culture, including various sectors and activities	Competency for cultural affairs has been transferred from the national level to the communities However, the "bi-cultural institutions" in Brussels (neither Flemish nor French) remain under federal authority	----	Cultural affairs major competency of the Communities (both legislative and executive power) Competency of the Communities applies within the territorial determined linguistic areas and for cultural institutions in Brussels, which belong to one of the two linguistic groups Communities set up, run and finance cultural institutions Support of cultural creativity and artistic activities Competency for Cultural affairs includes external cultural policy, cooperation between the Communities for the joint-interest-representation in international organisation	Participation in Cultural activities in the framework of local self-administration Only limited influence on the policy shaping

2.1.3 Germany

Characteristics	Federal Government	Regional Government - Länder	Local Government
Constitutional guarantee of freedom of arts (art. 5 BL) Financing of public cultural institutions (museums, archives, orchestras etc.), providing support for private cultural institutions and private associations taking over public tasks ("*freie Träger*") Large variety of museums, theatres, galleries, orchestras etc.	Competency for external cultural policy Provides the framework for the Goethe-Institute (public network of mediation and representation of German culture abroad) External Cultural Policy and representation of Germany in the EU Transnational cultural cooperation (both the federal level and the Länder are active) Legislation on press and film Provision of financial support for the protection of cultural heritage, for specific cultural projects and cultural institutions Limited competency for setting up and financing cultural institutions, which are of central relevance (e.g. national exhibition hall)	General competency of the Länder for cultural affairs, both legislative and executive power ("*Kulturhoheit*") Federal constitutional court emphasized that competency of the Länder for cultural affairs is a major element of their statehood Länder have set up and finance and co-finance various cultural institutions (theatres, museums, orchestras) Transnational cultural cooperation (both the Länder and the federal level are active)	Local level is particular active in the policy field of Culture Main responsibility for implementation of cultural activities is located on the local level, activities and policies on the local level vary according to policy orientation and the availability of financial means Financing of cultural institutions and events Both provision of financial support for private players and associations and setting up and running of public cultural institutions Local museums, theatres, cultural events, orchestras etc.

2.2 Regionalised States

2.2.1 France

Characteristics	National Government	Regional Authorities – Régions	Local Authorities – Départements / Communes
Conservation and protection of cultural objects (monuments, historic buildings, theatres, arts)	National level provides legal framework for those active in the policy field of Culture	General obligation to protect cultural heritage and monuments, most of the further activities in the policy field of Culture based on voluntary commitment	Obligations in the field of Culture are limited, however general obligation to protect cultural heritage and monuments
Constitutional guarantee of equal access to culture	External Cultural Policy is a competency of the national level		Départements are in charge of public Libraries
Provision of financial support to institutions and people active in Culture	Protection and conservation of cultural heritage of national relevance	Setting up and maintaining of archives (shared competency of the régions, départements and communes)	Setting up an maintaining of archives (shared competency of the régions, départements and communes)
Culture should contribute to the shaping of the national identity and promote regional and local cultural development	Obligation to guarantee equal access to cultural institutions	Setting up and running of cultural institutions, such as museums, libraries etc. (shared competency of the régions, départements and communes)	Local level devotes 1% of its budget to the acquisition of arts
	Most activities of the national level in the policy field of Culture are based on voluntary commitment		Competency to set up and run cultural institutions, as for example museums (shared competency of the régions, départements and communes)

2.2.2 Italy

Characteristics	National Government	Regional Authorities – Regions	Local Authorities	
			Provinces	Municipalities
Support public knowledge of European History Protection of cultural heritage Support non-commercial cultural exchange, artistic and literary activities Main instrument is public sponsorship	Setting of main objectives, central priorities and policy guidelines Provision of legal framework for policy field of Culture and cultural activities	Competency of running museums Responsibility for the protection of Cultural heritage Setting up of Cultural Centres Wide range of regional activities in the policy field of Culture, Regions act as sponsor for cultural activities Overlapping competency with local authorities	Setting up and running of cultural institutions (museums, galleries, orchestras) and information centres Overlapping competencies between regions, provinces and municipalities	Running of public libraries Overlapping competencies between regions, provinces and municipalities

According to the recent state reform in Italy (Law on Federalism, March 2001), the responsibility for museums and public libraries within the regions are determined as explicit competency of the regions within the framework set by the national government and parliament. The state reform has been approved by 64.2% of the voters in a political referendum in October 2001. However, the political consequences of the state reform for the political practice in the policy field of Culture remain to be seen.

2.2.3 Portugal

Characteristics	National Government	Regional Authorities		Local Authorities	
		Autonomous regions	Districts / Regional Boards of National Ministries	Municipalities	Parishes
Providing political framework for and setting up cultural institutions (theatres, museums, archives etc.)	Policy guidelines, central aims and general orientation for the policy field of Culture	Autonomous regions have competency to implement own cultural activities as far as their specific character and status are concerned		Setting up and running of cultural institutions (theatres, museums, libraries etc.)	Participation in the municipal policy making via programming contracts
Conservation of customs and conservation of cultural heritage	Legal framework for Cultural activities	For continental Portugal, the implementation of national policy objectives, programmes and cultural activities remains with the districts / regional boards of the national ministers			
Significant influence of catholic church in the political practice and in cultural activities	Responsibility for the protection of the national cultural heritage				
In the past focus on cultural capital Lisbon (1994), world exhibition (1998)					

2.2.4 Spain

Characteristics	National Government	Regional Authorities – Autonomous Communities (AC)	Local Authorities – Provinces and Municipalities
Policy field of Culture defined in a broad way, including radio, press, TV, arts, libraries, museums, monuments, sports etc. Spanish constitutional court uses broad definition of culture Support development of cultural activities	Provision of legal framework for Cultural activities Rules for press, film, radio and TV, furthermore for the protection of Spanish arts against exportation Running of state museums, central libraries and archives National institute for cinematography and audiovisual arts Protection of national cultural heritage, specific focus on the protection of cultural heritage in the overall public activities in the field of culture Responsibility for external cultural policy, cultural cooperation and representation of Spanish Culture abroad Promotion of fine arts	Competency for regulating artisanship, regional museums, libraries, monuments of regional interest, regional languages and sports Participation in cross-border cultural cooperation	Participation in Cultural activities in the context of the right of local self administration Framework for local activities in the policy field of Culture is regulated by national legislation and the statutes of the Autonomous Communities

2.2.5 United Kingdom

Characteristics	Central Government	Regional Authorities	Local Authorities
Policy field of Culture includes media, broadcasting, national heritage, libraries, museums, galleries, sports and tourism National lottery under authority of cultural department Provision of funding for those active in the policy field of Culture Cultural activities closely connected to tourism policy and sports	Setting of legal framework, provision of funding for public and private cultural institutions Regulation of broadcasting, media, arts, heritage, libraries, museums, sports, tourism, national lottery Political responsibility for the protection of the national cultural heritage Responsibility for external Cultural Policy Supervision of non-governmental, public bodies in the field of culture, media and sport, non-departmental public body for the protection of cultural heritage in England Responsibility for cultural institutions and events in England, development of regional focus in the cultural activities	*Scottish Parliament:* Primary legislative and executive power in the area of arts, funding of libraries and museums, financial support for cultural activities and institutions Executive agency responsible for monuments and historic buildings in Scotland *National Assembly for Wales:* Secondary legislative and executive power in the policy field of Culture, including public libraries, museums, sport, protection of Welsh language, conservation of historic buildings, funding of cultural institutions *Northern Ireland Assembly:* Responsibility for the policy field of Culture, including arts, libraries, museums, sports	Local authorities are important players in the delivery of cultural services, running of museums, support of tourism, arts and public libraries Close work relationship between national department and local authorities Development of Local Cultural Strategies corresponding to local needs National department and the Local Government Association monitor the policy implementation

Characteristics	Central Government	Regional Authorities	Local Authorities
		English Regional Development Agencies (RDAs)	
		Regional Arts Boards: Allocation of funds in England	
		Participation in the implementation of cultural activities and programmes in England	
		Government Offices for the Regions (GOR):	
		Coordination and participation in policy implementation, management of funding programmes in England	

2.3 Decentralised States

2.3.1 Denmark

Characteristics	National Government	Regional Level (counties – "amter")	Local Level (municipalities – "kommuner")
Policy field of Culture includes the protection of the national cultural heritage, running of or supervision of archives, libraries, media, museums, theatres, setting of legal framework for music, radio, TV and sports Principle of "cultural democracy" / community building-function Explicit focus in public cultural activities on the protection of cultural heritage	Setting of legal framework for cultural activities Provision of funding for cultural institutions Organisation and maintenance of archives, museums, research libraries Laying down of statutes and regulations for cultural institutions Responsibility for the protection of the cultural heritage International cultural cooperation National Arts Council (in charge of detailed regulation and supervision)	Indirect role in the policy field of Culture by the representation in sectoral committees Participation in the implementation of cultural initiatives decided at the national level Allocation of funds (shared competency of the regional and local level)	Indirect role in the policy field of Culture by the representation in sectoral committees Participation in the implementation of cultural initiatives decided at the national level Allocation of funds (shared competency of the regional and local level)

2.3.2 Finland

Characteristics	National Government	Regional Level - Provinces	Local Level
Service providing function of the state: Assure accessibility to cultural services and opportunity to participate in culture	Promoting and developing culture	13 regional arts councils, task of promoting professional and amateur arts	Receive state aid for public libraries
Activities in the policy field of Culture enacted as part of social policy	Arts Councils of Finland, subordinate to the national ministry of education in charge of the allocation of grants	Setting up and running of various cultural institutions (libraries, theatres, orchestras, museums)	Further cultural activities are optional for the local government
Culture and cultural activities with identity building function	Important role in the financing of cultural activities		Provision of wide range of cultural services
Central areas: folk music and folk dance	Bi-lateral cultural cooperation, cultural agreements with about 38 countries, e.g. Nordic Cultural Fund		Protection of cultural heritage
	Participation in the Council of Cultural Cooperation (CDCC) of the Council of Europe		Setting up of Centres for Culture and education
			Setting up and running of cultural facilities (libraries, museums, orchestras, concert halls)

2.3.3 The Netherlands

Characteristics	National Government	Regional Level – Provinces	Local Level – Muncipalities
Three dimensions of Culture Religious dimension: Protection of the freedom of religion, separation of state and church ("hands-off approach") Linguistic dimension: language education, specific policies for Friesland Arts and heritage dimension: no active, interventionist policy until the 1970s, since then: aim to assure access to culture for everyone, setting up of cultural institutions	Setting of general policy objectives for the policy field of Culture Provision of legal framework Arts centres in the provinces set up by the national level Competency for setting the policy framework for the protection of the national cultural heritage, policy formulation in the area of the protection of the national heritage dominated by the national government	Provide financial support for cultural activities under supervision of national government (financial reporting) Provinces received limited policy making power (coordination, stimulation of cultural supply) Provinces fulfil supervisory tasks with respect to policy implementation by the municipalities Provinces take part in the policy on the protection of the cultural heritage within the framework set by the national government	Provide financial support for cultural activities under supervision of national government (financial reporting), political role of the municipalities in the context of this role rather limited Policy implementation under supervision of the provinces and the national level Responsibility for maintaining cultural facilities (museums, etc.)

2.3.4 Sweden

Characteristics	National Government	Regional Level (counties – "län" / county councils "landsting")	Local Level (municipalities – "kommuner")
Culture as part of a popular movement: aim to assure access to cultural institutions for a broad public Public libraries as a top priority Only very limited activities in the field of cultural events and manifestos	Formulation of policy objectives for cultural activities and institutions Competency for setting the policy framework, central objectives and priorities in the area of the protection of the national cultural heritage, protection of cultural heritage is one essential national policy objective in the policy field of Culture Only limited number of objectives regulated by legislation (e.g. the public libraries in the Library Act)	Activities less regulated than in other policy fields Policy implementation in the field of Culture shared between the counties (län) and the local authorities Cultural activities of the counties (län) on the basis of a voluntary commitment Activities of the counties (län) in various cultural sectors (museums, theatres, orchestra etc.)	Activities less regulated than in other policy fields Cultural activities on the basis of a voluntary commitment Activities in various cultural sectors (museums, theatres, orchestra etc.), financial contribution of the local level in the policy field of Culture rather limited High degree of overlap in local activities and nationally set objectives

2.4 Two-Tiered States

2.4.1 Greece

Characteristics	National Government	Intermediary Institutions – Prefectures	Local Authorities – Municipalities
Public policy in the field of Culture includes archaeology, the protection of the national cultural heritage, the setting up of museums, archives, theatres, orchestras and libraries, music, fine arts A significant focus and priority in the political practice is laid on archaeology Beside this focus, broad range of cultural activities covered by the policy field of culture	Provides legal framework and policy guidelines Competency for the protection of arts and cultural heritage Supervisory function on a number of regional bodies, which implement cultural programmes and initiatives (e.g. institutions responsible for monuments and museums) Highly centralised structure in the field of archaeology (both with respect to policy formulation and implementation)	Support cultural development in their area (according to article 1 of the Code of Prefectural Government)	Local authorities can take a wide range of activities in the policy field of Culture (except archaeology), as for example music, fine arts, drama, regional cultural development Establishment of cultural centres, schools of music, dance or painting Running of libraries, museums, galleries etc.

2.4.2 Ireland

Characteristics	National Government	Geographic Regions - Provinces	Local Authorities – County Councils (and local authorities grouped around counties or large cities)
Culture and activities in the cultural sector not treated as separate policy field, but integrated in various other policy fields

Significant influence of the Roman Catholic Church on the policy field related to Culture

National government promotes culture by providing financial support and by setting the legal framework | Political responsibility for cultural affairs allocated on the national level

Provision of financial support, financing cultural activities is mainly allocated on the national level

Responsibility for the protection of cultural heritage

Competency for external cultural policy | --- | Local authorities implement increasingly own activities in the policy field of Culture

Setting up and running of theatres, cultural centres and libraries

Implementation of cultural initiatives, which are directly supported by the EU |

The Provinces are territorial entities within the Irish political system, which have, however, no regional power or policy responsibility within the policy field of Culture.

2.4.3 Luxembourg

Characteristics	National Government	Local Authorities – Municipalities
Political activities in the policy field of Culture focuses on providing the legal framework for those active in the arts sector Setting the organisational framework for cultural institutions Provision of subsidies Certain, specific cultural initiatives as for examples exhibitions on the history of Luxembourg	Political responsibility for cultural activities and programmes International cultural cooperation and external cultural policy Setting up and running of cultural institutions and infrastructure Coordination of national cultural centres Competency for the policy on the protection of the national cultural heritage Administration of Funds for national Cultural institutions	National level cooperates with the local authorities in the policy implementation Local level is in charge of the administration of support for cultural institutions (in cooperation with the national ministry)

3. *Public Health*

Public Health in a general, broad sense has been subject to community policies since 1958. Policies and activities were based on provisions for the free market for goods, as well as in the context of the policy for consumer protection. Since the beginning of the formulation of social policy guidelines and norms on the EU level, Public Health aspects have also been integrated in these policies, for example in the context of the programmes for security and health at work. With the reform implemented by the Single European Act, community competencies in the field of Public Health were further extended. Within the policies on environment, research and technology, the Public Health implications were explicitly recognized. In the context of the policy on environmental protection, a specific emphasis has been put on the protection of Public Health. The first community initiative in Public Health was the Community programme against cancer in 1986, which was based on a European Council decision.

Since the Treaty of Maastricht, Public Health has been introduced into the TEC as separate chapter and competency of the EC (art. 152 EC (ex-art. 129)). The regulation of Public Health confirmed the political practice. However, it constitutes also a new quality of the community policy in this area, as it introduced a legal basis for specific measures in the field of Public Health on community level. Since the Treaty of Amsterdam, the competency for setting binding quality and security standards for organs and blood given by a donor and the competency for setting binding regulations for veterinary medicine has been attributed to the EC. Furthermore, the cross-sector orientation of Public Health protection, which implies that Public Health is closely interrelated with other EC policies, was strengthened with the Treaty of Amsterdam, including an evaluation of the health protection in the community policies.

The EU policy field of Public Health, as regulated in article 152 EC (ex-art. 129), has the following main objectives: To guarantee a high level of health protection in the Community, the prevention of diseases and addictions, especially drug addictions, Public Health information and finally the support of research on infectious diseases. Given these objectives, the EC concentrates on promoting human health, the prevention of human diseases, the elimination of causes threatening human health, and the reduction of drug-related illnesses (including preventive and informative tasks). In recent years, a thematic focus on the protection against cancer, AIDS, the addiction to smoking, alcohol and drugs and the Health promotion and education can be identified. Community actions in Public Health are not restricted to a specific form as all forms for community actions as specified in art. 249 EC (ex-art. 189) may apply in the policy field of Public Health. However, the instruments of funding, recommendations, operational programs, and the establishment of networks are the most common forms. The cross-sectional clause ensures that health related matters must be accounted for in the formulation of other EU policies. The EC Health Policy furthermore includes the cooperation with third countries and international organisations in the area of Public Health, especially the WHO, the Council of Europe and the OECD (art. 152 3. EC (ex-art. 129 3.)). Additionally, the contribution to the attainment of a high level of health protection is included in the list of community objectives in art. 2 EC (ex-art. 2).

Public Health at EU level is closely interrelated and interconnected with other community policies. The main forms of these interrelations shall be summarised in this section. The most important legal basis for the interrelation of the policy field of Public Health with other policies is the cross-sector approach included in article 152 1. EC (ex-art. 129 1.), which obliges the EC to respect the protection of Public Health in all other community policies. The position of this cross-section-clause at the beginning of the provision on Public Health protection underlines its importance. Public Health protection does not only have to be taken into consideration, but the community activities must be directed towards a high standard of Public Health. The obligation to contribute to a high level of health protection applies to all EU organs and institutions. However, the EU institutions and organs retain a certain freedom in the assessment of this norm. Furthermore, the primary objective of a legal or political measure has to be taken into consideration.

Due to the historical development of the policy field of Public Health on the EU level, a close interrelation between Public Health and consumer protection and social policy has evolved. Within these policy fields, legal norms and political programmes have to be implemented in manner, which contributes to and assures a high level of health protection. In the field of social policy, for example, the setting of minimum health standards for workers and regulations on health at work has significant Public Health implications. Further interrelations exist with respect to the legal norms on the treatment of dangerous substances and pharmaceuticals. Furthermore Public Health is closely interrelated with the single market policy as far as the recognition of and trade with pharmaceuticals are concerned. These policies shall, according to the general policy guidelines, contribute to a high standard of Public Health protection. Additionally the environmental policy and measures for environmental protection shall contribute to the protection of Public Health and often have a direct impact on Public Health. Further links exist between Public Health and the Common Agricultural Policy, as well as to food and fisheries policy. The EU research and technology policy covers also medical research. Often, the implementation of health policy measures in the context of a specific policy objective requires activities in various EC policy fields. The policy against AIDS, for example, includes health education, prevention, research policy, the policy on pharmaceuticals, as well as the external cooperation with developing countries.

However, it is equally important to emphasize the limits of Community activities and the application of the principle of subsidiarity and additionality in the field of Public Health. Within the concept of the EU Public Health, the Member States responsibility for Public Health remains intact. Rather than replacing the national policies, the EC policy field of Public Health is designed to complement the national policies. As for other EC policies, the principle of subsidiarity applies. Therefore, the EU does not formulate an own, independent Health Policy, but contributes to the national policies. An additional limitation of Community policy in the field of Public Health is to be found in the prohibition of any harmonisation of legal and administrative forms for public health provision. Health care service and their provision, including the financing of public health services, remain under national political responsibility (art. 152 5. EC). In this context, some authors emphasise, that the Member States remain the "Master of public health policy" (Schwartze, p. 1566).

Comparing the EU approach to Public Health to the overall political agenda in the 15 EU Member States, it is characteristic that main priorities and activities in Public Health are mainly developed and decided on the national level within the EU Member States. The setting of the overall policy framework by the national government applies to federal, regionalised, decentralised and two-tiered states. Apparently, there is a strong tendency towards uniformity in the basic rules and priorities for Public Health in the Member States. The organisational aspects of the Public Health sector, the health insurance systems and further aspects of Public Health services are a central part of the national Public Health Policies. Therefore, the research team agreed to include these aspects in the tables, although they are not covered by the EU Public Health Policy. Similar to the other policy fields, this extension of the scope of analysis to the main, common characteristics aims at providing an improved overview on the policy field in the 15 Member States.

Within the framework set by national governments and administrations, specific programmes and activities are developed by the sub-national level. The tables on the different states will show that the leeway of the sub-national players to implement specific programmes is considerably higher in federal and regionalised states, compared to decentralised and two-tiered states. Especially in two-tiered states, the policy and the form of its implementation is almost exclusively decided by the national government and administration.

In Public Health, the cooperation of national governments with non-departmental public and private bodies is significantly higher than in other policy fields. The national governments cooperate in a close relationship with advisory agencies and associations.

3.1 Federal States

3.1.1 Austria

Characteristics	Federal Government	Regional Government - Länder	Local Government
The main objective is an optimal provision of public health services in a cost-effective way Political debate on cost-reduction National Health Plan regulates detailed planning of health care system Preventive measures focus on AIDS-prevention, prevention of addiction to alcohol, promotion of vaccination, the problem of antibiotic-resistances etc. Political debate focuses on institutional questions (organisational aspects of public health sector, health insurances and service provision) Hospital system rather separate from Public Health Compulsory health insurance, insurance based public health financing with public contributions	General political responsibility for main priorities and policy objectives of Public Health Provision of legal framework Definition of framework for policy implementation ("mittelbare Bundesverwaltung")	Far reaching regionalisation with respect to the hospital system Setting legal framework for hospital care Länder and private associations ("freie Träger") run hospitals, Länder are most important level for running the hospitals Länder take important share in financing hospitals Responsibility for policy implementation in accordance with the rules set by the federal level ("mittelbare Bundesverwaltung")	Local health services ("Gemeindesanitätsdienst") Local authorities run local hospitals ("Krankenhausträger")

147

3.1.2 Belgium

Characteristics	Federal Government	Regional Government		Local Government
		Regions	*Communities*	*Provinces / Municipalities*
Provision of public health care services and preventive care	Legislation on hospitals, home for elderly, psychiatric institutions, health & invalidity insurance, recognition of pharmaceuticals	No genuine regional competency	Elaboration and application of national law	General principle of local self-administration
Guarantee access to health care services		Competencies in related policy fields (e.g. environment, control of enterprises)	Formulation and implementation of policy on Public Health care services	Responsibility for public welfare services (psychological aid, medical corps)
Organisation of emergency service	Rules for medical, nursing and paramedical professions		Communities are running the hospitals and provide public health care	Administrative control and responsibilities with respect to public hospitals
Medical policy (recognition, prices, reimbursement of pharmaceuticals)	Social security and grants for invalid persons			
Structure and financing of hospital system	Agency for security of the food chain		Policy towards invalid and elderly (except for federal competencies)	
Health insurance system	Provision of legal framework for health education		Communities are in charge of public health education / disease prevention	

3.1.3 Germany

Characteristics	Federal Government	Regional Government – Länder	Local Government
Central objective of Public Health is the provision of effective public health care system in a cost-effective way Public Health information and education, focus on provision of human organs given by a donor, provision of blood given by donor, health of children and young people, AIDS-prevention, prevention of addiction to drugs and alcohol Need for cost-reduction in public health sector 90% of the population covered by public health insurances Providing legal framework for organisations active in public health services	Public Health covered by concurrent legislative power (art. 70 BL) Sets the framework for the organisation and performance of the health sector Concurrent legislative power for prevention of infectious diseases, permission of medical goods, medical specialists, laws on chemicals, economic situation of hospitals, etc. Exclusive legislative power for social affairs Health education and information fulfilled by the federal agency for health education ("*Bundeszentrale für Gesundheitliche Aufklärung*")	Public Health covered by concurrent legislative power (art. 70 BL) Legislation on medical corps ("*Gesundheitsdienst*"), rescue service, organisational matters of the hospitals Implementation of preventive measures in the health sector (action programmes etc.)	Health Policy implementation remains decentralised Local medical corps ("*Gesundheits-ämter*") Local level enjoys right of self-administration Running and financing of communal hospitals Communal programmes for promoting public Health

3.2 Regionalised States

3.2.1 France

Characteristics	National Government	Regional Authorities – Régions	Local Authorities – Départements / Communes
Protection of Public Heath, protection against illnesses

Security at work

Specific focus and priority on organisational matters of the health sector and health insurance system

Public Health includes physical, mental and social dimension

Insurance based public health reimbursement scheme | General policy guidelines and objectives

Providing of legal framework for Health Policy

Regulation of financial and legal aspects related to the public health insurance system

Formulation and implementation of specific programmes in the field of public health education (cancer, AIDS) | Public health planning, for example with respect to Public Health services, facilities and hospitals

Setting up of public health programmes | Provision of public health services

Supervision of non-governmental bodies active in Health Policy

Promotion of vaccination, protection against infectious diseases

Organisation and financing of medical centres and services

Social assistance for handicapped people, public health education, assistance to families, children and elderly

Municipal sanitary rule |

3.2.2 Italy

Characteristics	National Government	Regional Authorities – Regions	Local Authorities	
			Provinces	Municipalities
Protection of Public Health as important public policy objective in the constitution	Definition of main policy objectives and guidelines for Public Health	Legislative and executive competency in the field of Public Health	Participation in the administration of Public Health in the context of the constitutional principle of local self administration	Participation in the administration of Public Health in the context of the constitutional principle of local self administration
Extensive scope of public health protection	Provision of legal framework for general principles for Public Health	Obligation to respect the general principles laid down by the national government	Running of public health services	Running of public health services
Public Health information and education, disease prevention	Provision of legal framework for public health services	Planning and organisation of public Health sector and public health services	Responsibility for the planning of local public health facilities	Overlapping responsibilities between provinces and municipalities
Compulsory Public Health insurance system, contributions to public health insurance by employers and employees		Regions adopt and implement sanitary plans	Overlapping responsibilities between provinces and municipalities	Expenditures for public health covers about 30% of the total municipal expenditures
		Responsibility for initiating and implementing health policy projects, different regional priorities for health education and disease prevention		

151

In the recent constitutional reform (March 2001), the competency for Public Health services and hospitals has been transferred to the regions. Within their sphere of competency, the regions have to respect general principles and guidelines as laid down by the national level or by other regions. The reform has been approved by 64.2% of the voters in a referendum in October 2001. As for the other policy fields examined in this study, the political implications of the constitutional reform remain to be seen.

3.2.3 Portugal

Characteristics	National Government	Regional Authorities		Local Authorities	
		Autonomous regions	*Districts / Regional Boards of National Ministries*	*Municipalities*	*Parishes*
Central policy objective is the aim and efforts to improve public health standards Definition of standards and principles for public health care (hospitals and medical services) Setting of general rules for health insurances Public health information and education	Policy guidelines and objectives set by the national government Supervision of health sector Provision of legal framework for the compulsory health insurance system	Autonomous Regions Azores and Madeira are competent for regulating Public Heath Policy and Services as far as their specific status and autonomy are concerned For continental Portugal, the respective administrative tasks of Public Health Policy coordination remain with the districts / regional boards of the national ministries		Setting up local health centres Running public health services Public Health education	Setting up local health centres Running public health services Public Health education

153

3.2.4 Spain

Characteristics	National Government	Regional Authorities – Autonomous Communities (AC)	Local Authorities – Provinces and Municipalities
Policy field of Public Health covers:	Provision of legal framework for Public Health	Implementation of national public health legislation	Environmental health control
Public Health education	Definition of overall health policy objectives	Regulating power for regional planning and management of Public Health	Environmental aspects of health care
Prevention of illnesses	Legislation on pharmaceutical products		
Public Health services	National Ministry of Health and National Institute of Public Health Care in charge of policy formulation	Public Health care has been transferred to certain AC, provision of health care services within the AC (Catalonia, Andalusia, Basque Country, Valencia)	
Health insurance system	Social security and social services regulated on national level (Ministry of Labour and Social security)	Public Health education: Setting up of public health centres on the AC's level	
Organisational aspects of social security	Administration of social security system by National Health Institute (Instituto Nacional de SALUD, INSALUD), Instituto de Migraciones y Servicios Sociales (IMSERSO) administers complementary services in the framework of social security	Competencies of the national institutes of SALUD and IMSERSO (see column on national government) have been transferred to AC with higher level of autonomy	

3.2.5 United Kingdom

Characteristics	Central Government	Regional Authorities	Local Government
Main policy objective is the continuing improvement of Public Health Policy field of Public Health includes health education, combating illnesses, the insurance system, regulations on hospitals and food standards Health care reimbursement scheme based on health insurance system, both public and private health insurances	General policy guidelines, legislative framework and setting of overall policy objectives for Public Health Legislation on and implementation of Public Health Policy for England National Government in charge of public health education in England, Health Agency in charge of specific aspects and programmes of health education and disease prevention	*Scottish Parliament:* Health Policy has been devolved to the regional government and parliament (primary legislative power) Administration of Health services / hospitals and health education in Scotland *National Assembly for Wales:* Secondary legislative and executive powers for public health matters Competency covers also health education and health care services (including hospitals) Executive Agency for health promotion in Wales *Northern Ireland Assembly:* Policy field of Public Health has been devolved to the Northern Ireland Assembly and government Competency of the regional government for health education, health policy and health services / hospitals, non-departmental, public body in charge of health promotion programmes	Local government activities in the field of Public Health are based on government legislation and statutes Public Health care provision Local authorities work in partnership with hospitals in their area to promote public health Health care for elderly, children and handicapped people Local authorities take part in the Public Health education and preventive care with respect to specific public health issues (cancer, AIDS etc.)

Characteristics	Central Government	Regional Authorities	Local Government
		Regional Development Agencies (RDAs):	

3.3 Decentralised States

3.3.1 Denmark

Characteristics	National Government	Regional Level (counties – "amter")	Local Level (municipalities – "kommuner")
Organisation and legal framework for health provision, health personnel recruitment, hospitals and pharmacies, pharmaceuticals, vaccinations etc.	Preparation of legislation on Public Health	Ownership, organisation and maintenance of public hospital system	Supervisory authority for personnel providing the care for the elderly and school dentists
	Setting of policy guidelines for health care system	Health policy central responsibility of the counties	
	Setting up programmes for training of health care personnel	Responsibility for hospitals accounts for 60% of the total county councils expenditures	
Health care is free of charge, expenditures of Public Health are covered by tax revenues	Control of foodstuff	Counties obliged by national legislation to guarantee free medical treatment	
	Regulation of general budgetary conditions related to Public Health and public health services	Setting up of health care plans, including health education and disease prevention priorities	

3.3.2 Finland

Characteristics	National Government	Regional Level - Provinces	Local Level
Focus and emphasis on equal availability of health services Constitutional, subjective right of the citizens to health services Main areas of the policy field of Public Health: Health care reimbursement scheme, health and social services, preventive health care and health protection at work Health services free of charge, covered by tax revenues, cost-cutting pressure In recent years, discussion on privatisation, small private sector of public health services	Legislative framework for and policy objective of Health Policy Relatively close steering in the 1970s / 1980s, since then, decrease of national influence In recent years, dismantling of national laws and regulations, increased freedom for the local level	Supervisory power on public health services	Responsibility for providing health care services Service providing function of the municipalities in Public Health (e.g. Municipal health centres) Small municipalities use possibility to set up inter-municipal authorities Freedom of action for the local level has been significantly increased in recent years For specialised care, 21 hospital districts have been set up, each municipality belongs to a district, representative of the municipality in the hospital district administration

3.3.3 The Netherlands

Characteristics	National Government	Regional Level - Provinces	Local Level – Muncipalities
Policy field of Public Health has been strongly influenced by "pillarisation" of society: Dual hospital system (public and church-based)	Policy framework, legislation and regulations on specific aspects of Public Health provided by the national level	Limited scope for setting own priorities in the implementation of Public Health Policy	In charge of social and preventive health care on the local level (municipal medical services)
Health policy is dealt with under the rules of consociational democracy	Legal and political framework for Public Health education provided by the national government	Supervisory role concerning availability, distribution and planning of medical facilities (e.g. hospitals)	Limited role of the municipalities in the policy implementation
Health Policy dominated by players on the national level	Health inspection	Advisory function for setting priorities for public health planning	Participation in regional overviews (see provinces)
State fixes common quality standards for all medical facilities	Financial resources of health care facilities are provided by the national government	Preparation of regional public health plans on public health, involving the local health care institutions and municipalities	Municipal role in public health is of great importance for the citizens, but closely linked to the national policy making
Non-interventionist policy of the public authorities with respect to church-based sector		Monitor and implement national Health Policy	Minor financial contribution to the public health financing by the Municipal Fund
Setting up of consultation services, ambulant services and preventive services		Licensing of ambulance service	
		Implementation of Public Health education, provision of public health education services	

3.3.4 Sweden

Characteristics	National Government	Regional Level (counties – "län" / county councils - "landsting")	Local Level (municipalities – "kommuner")
Long tradition of the policy field of Public Health, similar to the other Scandinavian countries High status of Public Health on the political agenda Policy field covers the aspects of disease prevention and health promotion, the regulation Health insurance system and the hospitals Cross-sector approach to Public Health, having significant influence on various related policy fields, e.g. environmental policy Health promotion and education similar to the WHO approach expressed in the "Health for all programme"	Formulation of policy objectives and guidelines, focus on general guidelines rather than on close policy steering Preparation of legislation on Public Health and provision of legal framework for Public Health Setting of legal framework for health insurance system 2 national boards related to Public Health: National Institute of Public Health, National Board of Health and Welfare (supervision of medical care and social services)	Counties implement national legislation on Public Health Counties develop comprehensive health reports and programmes Counties take part in the implementation of Health promotion and disease prevention programmes Counties enjoy considerable freedom of action for the regional authorities About 80% of the Counties' expenditures are related to Public Health	Participation in the implementation of Public Health Policy Setting up of public health planners and public health committees: planning of local public health service supply Considerable freedom of action for the local authorities

3.4 Two-Tiered States

3.4.1 Greece

Characteristics	National Government	Intermediary Institutions I - Regions	Intermediary Institutions II - Prefectures	Local Authorities – Municipalities
Policy field of Public Health in the national context covers two main dimensions: National Health System (setting up and regulation of hospitals) and National System of Social Care (programmes for health promotion and disease prevention, focus on AIDS victims, drug and alcohol addiction and other public health issues) **Focus in Public Health on hospital system** National system of social care: insurance based public health reimbursement scheme Public Health Programmes with a similar approach as the EU programmes Significant influence of the church in the provision of Public Health services and medical care	Formulation of policy guidelines, general standards and legal framework Public Health education and disease prevention Definition of legal framework and policy guidelines for public health services Participation in the policy implementation, supervisory power on public health service provision, currently discussions on the decentralisation of these services (see below)	-----	-----	Involved in providing first grade health care Large municipalities also provide preventive medicine Overall contribution of the local level to Public Health rather limited

161

Recent reform proposals put forward by the national Health Ministry (July 2000) proposes a moderate decentralisation in the policy field of Public Health. Beside the responsibility of the national government, a 'Regional Health System' shall be established in each region as a public law body. The Regional Health system will include all units of the region (hospitals, health centres etc.). The Regional Health System will remain subordinate to the national ministry. The Regional Health System will be competent for coordination, specialisation and implementation of Public Health Policy in the region, for drafting the "Entreprenurial Health Action Plan, for the approval of the health units' budget and for a wide range of internal, organisational matters.

3.4.2 Ireland

Characteristics	National Government	Geographic Regions - Provinces	Local Authorities – County Councils (and local authorities grouped around counties or large cities)
Comparatively low priority of Public Health, other policies have higher status on political agenda Dependency on the UK for certain specialist care services National Health Policy influenced by EU policies and programmes Significant influence of the Catholic Church on the provision of public health services Public Health reimbursement scheme based on health insurance	Public Health competency of the national government National government in charge of setting up the legal and organisational framework for the hospital system National government is in charge of public health education and disease prevention programmes; in recent years, increased attention has been given to this sector of Public Health Agencies on the local level are set up and controlled by the national level and deal with specialist aspects of medical care. Agencies are still setting legal framework and policy guidelines for health insurance system	----	Running and implementation of Health Policy programmes (both national and EU-programmes Implementation of measures related to Public Health Programmes

The provinces are traditional territorial entities within the Irish political system, which have, however, no regional power or policy responsibility within the policy field of Public Health.

3.4.3 Luxembourg

Characteristics	National Government	Local Authorities – Municipalities
Organisation of health sector Supervision of the hospital system, elaboration of hospital plans Public Health education Improvement of preventive medicine, pro-active drug policy	Providing legal framework on public care professions, medical schools, supervision on preventive and social medicine Re-education services and services for mentally handicapped persons, setting legal framework for institutions related to public health care Specialised Public Health Direction is in charge of studies related to public health issues, advisory functions, task of monitoring legislation National administration supervises public health service provision	Participation in the day-to-day management of policies related to Public Health Administrative tasks related to the policy implementation

4. Transeuropean Networks

The policy on guidelines and actions in the field of Transeuropean Networks (transport, telecommunications and energy) has been introduced into the framework of Community policies by the Treaty of Maastricht (Treaty on the European Union, TEU).

The policy field of Guidelines and Actions for the Construction and Expansion of Trans-European Networks is regulated in art. 154 – 156 EC (ex-art. 129 B – ex-art. 129 D). To achieve the objectives as laid down in art. 14 EC (ex-art. 7 A) (Internal Market) and art. 158 EC (ex-art. 130 A) (Economic and Social Cohesion), the European Community contributes to the establishment and development of Trans-European Networks in the areas of transport, telecommunications and energy infrastructures. According to art. 154 EC (ex-art. 129 B), the TEN shall enable citizens of the Union, economic operators and regional and local communities to derive the full benefits from an area without internal frontiers. This is the only explicit reference to regional and local authorities in the TEC. Trans-European in this context means national networks which are inter-connected over national frontiers and which serve to fulfil EU objectives (art. 14 and 158 EC).

According to art. 155 EC (ex-art. 129 C), EU measures for building TEN are establishing guidelines covering objectives, priorities and general principles for measures envisaged. The guidelines identify projects of common interest. Additionally, the EU implements measures to ensure the interoperability of networks, particularly in the field of technical standardisation, supports projects of common interest co-financed by Member States through feasibility studies, loan guarantees or interest-rate subsidies. The Community can also contribute to the financing of specific projects through the Cohesion Fund (i.e. Spain, Portugal, Greece, Ireland). In financial terms, transport is by far the most important part of TEN. The establishment of Transeuropean Networks in the area of energy, telecommunications, harbours and waterways, as well as airports and telematic systems is of significantly lower priority in the EU context and on the political agenda of the EU. Therefore, the research team concentrates on transport projects in the road- and railway sector. The European Council in Cardiff of May 1998 has agreed on 14 priority Transeuropean Network projects for the planning period until 2006, to which the research team will make specific reference in the tables on the Member States[5]. It should be noted that this reference to the priority transport projects reflects a concentration on the main, central policies and projects.

A central objective of the EU policy is the support of the interoperability of national infrastructures. Therefore, the EU supports investment in and the extension and improvement of existing networks. The EU policy aims at closing gaps in the networks and supporting access to national networks (technical standards, legal questions, no market regulation).

It has already been analysed in the context of the sections on the previous policy fields, that policy-making and the different policy fields of mandatory consultation are closely interrelated and interconnected. Similar

---

[5] Information based on: European Commission: 14 TEN priority projects, http://www.europa.eu.int/comm/transport/themes/network/english/tentpp9807/tentpp9807.html

observations can be made for the policy field of Transeuropean Networks. Firstly, and probably most importantly, the policy on the establishment of and investment in Transeuropean Networks is closely interrelated with the single market policy. TEN shall contribute to the aim of making full profit of the single market. Regional and local level shall have most effective benefit from single market, to which the TEC makes explicit reference. The concept of TEN identifies major infrastructure connections within the EU as an essential precondition for an effective benefit from the single market. Without the investment in infrastructure, a fluent exchange of goods and services is not possible. Investment in transport infrastructure is a precondition for the free movement of people and workers. The interrelated policy fields of TEN and the single market aim at establishing an open competition. Beside the close interrelation with the single market objective and policy, the policy field of TEN is closely interconnected with the EU policy and regulation on public subsidies and the EU competition law.

Furthermore, the policy of TEN is linked to the EU objective of economic and social cohesion, to which the article 155 EC (ex-art. 129 C) makes explicit reference. Regional and Structural Policy and the policy on the establishment of Transeuropean Networks both aim at supporting the economic development and prosperity of the respective region. The interrelation of both policy fields can furthermore be illustrated by the financing of TEN projects, with major TEN projects being financed by the Cohesion Fund. The interrelation of policies for the economic development is furthermore inherent in the underlying objective in these policies, which aim at coordinating the different policies for the economic development.

Furthermore, the policy field of TEN is interrelated with environmental policy (art. 174 EC (ex-art. 130 R)). The emphasis on sustainable mobility and environmental-friendly forms of transport is a typical characteristic of the interrelation of these two policy fields and the significant influence of environmental policy objectives on the planning and implementation of TEN projects. Finally, an intersection of TEN projects with the EU Transport Policy has to be mentioned, with TEN projects aiming at supporting common objectives in transport policy. Beside these various interrelations and intersections, it seems necessary to point to the fact that TEN as such are a genuine EU policy with an own legal basis.

Similar to the other policy fields examined, the policy on TEN is bound by certain restrictions. Additionally, the principle of subsidiarity applies. Within the limited competency transferred to the EU in the policy field of TEN, not all infrastructure projects are covered. Especially infrastructure projects with only regional and / or local implications are excluded from the policy framework of TEN. Furthermore, the article on the establishment of TEN mentions the applicable forms of TEN projects, that means other forms of transnational, European infrastructure projects, outside the policy areas mentioned above, are excluded from the policy framework of TEN. Furthermore, it is important to emphasise the non-exclusive character of the EU policy, with TEN projects constituting only a contribution to national policies. Infrastructure policy remains a primary responsibility of the Member States, especially with respect to the planning and implementation of projects. The EU fulfils only an additional and complementary function in this policy field. The function of the EU is furthermore limited by the focus on the interrelation of the

Member States and the support of the interconnection and interoperability of the national infrastructure.

The comparative analysis of the political responsibility for Transeuropean Networks and the respective national policy fields of road- and railway infrastructure, telecommunications and energy clearly demonstrates a dominance of the national political level, government and parliament, in the 15 Member States. In all Member States, the political responsibility and legislative competency for the respective policy field lies with the national level. In the federal and regionalised states, the sub-national level has important functions in the implementation of major infrastructure projects and is generally consulted in the planning phase, however, these tasks of implementation are characterised by a comparatively close steering of the national level. The freedom for setting own priorities by the regional and local level is rather limited. In decentralised and especially in two-tiered states, the policy on major transport infrastructures, telecom and energy projects are almost exclusively a matter of the national government. Although regions might have an important interest in this policy field, their channels of access are rather limited. Therefore, the CoR might play an important role in this respect, providing an alternative channel for political access. Transeuropean Networks are an important factor for the economic development on the regional level, which explains the vital interest, especially of the peripheral regions in this policy field.

For the areas of telecommunications and energy, some general characteristics shall be mentioned. As stated above, the research team concentrated on the transport infrastructure, as this is the policy area with most EU activities in the framework of TEN. Similarly, most members of the regional offices interviewed in the context of the project underlined that transport infrastructure projects are of much higher importance than energy- and telecom-infrastructure projects. In almost all Member States, the sectors of energy and telecommunications are currently in a process of market liberalisation and privatisation of the formerly state owned companies. In all Member States, the remaining regulatory power is attributed to the national level, with the regional and local level having only limited channels of access. Taking this characteristic into consideration, the research team has decided not to include energy and telecom in the following tables on TEN, which deal with the share and distribution of competencies between the different levels of government.

4.1 Federal States

4.1.1 Austria

Characteristics	Federal Government	Regional Government - Länder	Local Government
Transport infrastructure planning guided by environmental aspects Underlying aim of the reduction of road transport Support of environmental friendly forms of transport (e.g. combined transport, application of the real-cost-principle) Connection of peripheral regions to the main transport axis'	Planning and construction of major transport infrastructure under federal responsibility, policy guidelines set by the federal government Planning is attributed to joint-stock-company (*"Autobahn- und Schnellstraßen-finanzierungsgesellschaft"*) Planning and construction of railway infrastructure is attributed to the federal level Construction and maintenance of railway infrastructure attributed to specialised joint-stock company (*"Österreichische Bundesbahn / Hochleistungsstrecken AG"*)	Consultation rights in the planning procedure of road and railway infrastructure projects, participation in the detailed planning Limited margin of action in the context of administration of railway and road infrastructure projects (*"mittelbare Bundesverwaltung"*)	Consultation rights in the planning procedure of road- and railway infrastructure projects, limited influence on the location of tracks Participation in the detailed planning of major infrastructure projects

Austria takes part in the priority transport project for the establishment of TEN number 1, establishing a high-speed train from Berlin to Nürnberg and München to Verona, with the section directly affecting Austria being Munich – Kufstein (total investment €32 million), Kufstein - Innsbruck (€1,610 million) and Innsbruck – Fortezza (€3,800 million).

4.1.2 Belgium

Characteristics	Federal Government	Regional Government		Local Government
		Regions	*Communities*	*Provinces / Municipalities*
Focus on investment in railway infrastructure	General decision-making power	Transport infrastructure planning	-----	Consultation rights in the planning process
Aim to support sustainable mobility	Setting of political priorities	Detailed planning for all transport infrastructure projects		Regulation of technical aspects of transport infrastructure planning and construction
Transport infrastructure planning both on the federal level and the level of the regions	Determination of financial conditions for the investment			
Interrelation of the policy field of transport infrastructure with environmental policy, economic development, social and fiscal policy	Decisions on the Belgian participation in TEN			

Within the EU, Belgium can be considered as one of the centres for TEN High speed train connections (e.g. Brussels - London, Brussels – Paris, Antwerp – Amsterdam, Brussels – Köln). Belgium benefits especially from project no. 2 of the TEN priority transport projects establishing a high speed train connection Paris – Bruxelles – Köln, with a total investment in Belgium of €4,258 million. Transeuropean Networks for Transport have been closely integrated into the national infrastructure policy and the national investment plans.

4.1.3 Germany

Characteristics	Federal Government	Regional Government - Länder	Local Government
Trade and export orientated country Transport infrastructure is considered as prerequisite for economic growth Guiding principle of sustainable mobility, support of combined transport Increased public investment in railway infrastructure Within the framework of TEN: Focus on east-west road- and railway connections	Planning and construction of road infrastructure is covered by the concurrent legislative power according to art. 72 / 74 of the German Constitution Only certain roads under federal authority ("*Bundesfernstraßen und Bundesautobahnen*") TEN projects mainly under federal responsibility, close cooperation with the Länder in the implementation Exclusive legislative power of the federal level for the planning and construction of railway infrastructure (art. 73 / 74 I Nr. 23 BL) Policy implementation and administrative competency in the railway sector (art. 87 e BL)	Länder take over tasks in the implementation of major transport infrastructure projects Detailed planning and construction of transport infrastructure under Länder responsibility	Consultation rights in the planning process Cooperation with the Länder in the detailed planning

173

TEN Priority Projects in Germany:

Being especially affected by the increased transport in the EU, Germany has been identified as an important country for the establishment of TEN. The following TEN priority transport projects cover infrastructure investment in Germany:

> Priority transport project No. 1, establishing a high speed train connection including combined transport for the North-South direction, running from Berlin, via Halle/Leipzig, Erfurt to Nürnberg and from München to Verona, with the total investment in Germany amounting to €9,067 million (with investment of €1,693 million Berlin Lehrter train station, €1,387 million Berlin-Halle/Leipzig, €2,287 million, Halle/Leipzig – Erfurt €2,287 million, Erfurt –Nürnberg €3,668 million and München – Kufstein €32 million).

> Priority transport project No. 2, establishing a high speed train from Paris, via Bruxelles, Köln/Frankfurt, Amsterdam to London and covering a total investment in Germany of €4,318 million.

> Priority transport project No. 4, establishing a High Speed Train line from Paris, via Reims and Metz to Mannheim, Strasbourg and Luxembourg. The total investment in the Germany amounts to €459 million.

4.2 Regionalised States

4.2.1 France

Characteristics	National Government	Regional Authorities – Régions	Local Authorities – Départements / Communes
Transport infrastructure is characterised as prerequisite for economic development Transport infrastructure as part of the overall economic policy, supporting economic development and growth	Policy formulation and general policy guidelines for public infrastructure Implementation of major road infrastructure projects	Participation in the planning and implementation of concrete projects	---

France is covered by several of the 14 TEN priority transport projects establishing and upgrading major transport infrastructure lines in the EU:

Priority transport project No. 2, establishing a High Speed Train line from Paris, via Bruxelles, Köln/Frankfurt, Amsterdam to London. This infrastructure projects has been completed in 1996.

Priority transport project No. 3, establishing a High Speed Train connection from Madrid to the French border near Dax and from Madrid via Zaragoza, Barcelona to Montpellier, with the total investment amounting to €1,494 million.

Priority transport project No. 4, establishing a High Speed Train from Paris, via Reims and Metz to Mannheim, and Strasbourg and Luxembourg, with a total investment in France of €4,218 million.

Priority transport project No. 6, establishing a High Speed Train / Combined Transport line from Lyon, via Torino, Milano, Verona, Venezia to Trieste, with the investment for the section Lyon-Montmelian and Montmelian-Torino amounting to €8,600 million.

4.2.2 Italy

Characteristics	National Government	Regional Authorities – Regions	Local Authorities	
			Provinces	*Municipalities*
Transport infrastructure is characterised as prerequisite for economic development Focus on railway and highway construction In the EU context, tendency to use a wide concept of TEN	Legislative and executive competency for major road infrastructure projects	Competency for planning and construction of railways and motorways of regional interest, this might affect TEN Policy implementation, detailed planning	Participation in the implementation of transport infrastructure projects in the context of the principle of local self administration Competency for road maintenance Overlapping responsibilities between provinces and municipalities	Participation in the implementation of transport infrastructure projects in the context of the principle of local self administration Responsibility for spatial planning and development Overlapping responsibilities between provinces and municipalities

In the recent state reform of March 2001, the competency for city planning, the regional railway and road system and harbours has been attributed to the regions. The constitutional reform has been approved in a referendum in October 2001 by 64.2% of the voters. Therefore, the consequences of the reform for the political practice remain to be seen.

Italy is directly affected by several of the TEN priority transport projects established and developed on the EU level:

> Priority transport project No. 1, establishing a high speed train from Berlin to Nürnberg and from München to Verona, with the total investment for the section Innsbruck – Fortezza amounting to €3,800 million and Fortezza –Verona €625 million.

> Priority transport project No. 6, establishing a high-speed train / combined transport line from Lyon to Trieste, with a total investment of €7,000 million for the section Montméllian – Torino, €2,600 million for Torino – Milano, €2,400 million for Milano – Verona, €1,900 million for Verona – Venezia and €1,900 million for the section Venezia – Trieste.

> Priority transport project No. 10, extending the Malpensa airport near Milano with a total investment of €1,047 million.

4.2.3 Portugal

Characteristics	National Government	Regional Authorities		Local Authorities	
		Autonomous regions	Districts / Regional Boards of National Ministries	Municipalities	Parishes
Dominance and preference for road transport, rising share of road transport Massive public investment in transport infrastructure to cope with rise of transport Transport axis follow coastal line Infrastructure policy not yet integrated policy covering all aspects of transport	Responsibility and legislative competency for construction and maintenance of road and railway infrastructure Cooperation with the local authorities in the planning process	Participation of the Regional Boards of the National Ministries in the administrative planning process Autonomous Regions do currently not take part in TEN, in case of TEN projects affecting the Autonomous regions (or similar major transport infrastructure projects), the regional governments possess consultation rights in the planning procedure		Participation in the planning process (detailed planning) in cooperation with national government	Participation in the planning process (detailed planning) in cooperation with national government

178

Of the 14 priority transport projects of Transeuropean Networks, project no. 8 is of central importance for Portugal, as it establishes a multimodal (rail and road) link in Portugal as well as between Portugal – Spain and Central Europe. The total investment in Portugal amounts to €1,809 million for the rail infrastructure and €1,737 million for the investment in road infrastructure.

Portugal receives additional support in the framework of the Cohesion Fund, which amounted between 1993 and 1999 to €1,446 million, including financial support for road construction of €856.3 million, railways €334 million, ports €95.8 million and airports €159.9 million.

4.2.4 Spain

Characteristics	National Government	Regional Authorities – Autonomous Communities (AC)	Local Authorities – Provinces and Municipalities
High degree of coherence between Spanish and EU understanding of transport infrastructure policy High priority to the investment in transport infrastructure Transport infrastructure is seen as central tool to support the economic development	Competency for legislation, planning and implementation almost exclusively allocated on the national level Competency for construction and maintenance of road- and railway infrastructure that run through more than one AC	Competency for planning and construction of transport infrastructure lines within the territory of the AC (railways and roads)	Framework for local activities in the implementation of major, national and EU infrastructure projects is regulated by national legislation and the statutes of the Autonomous Communities

Spain is covered by priority transport projects of TEN. These are the following:

Priority transport project No. 3, establishing a high-speed connection between Madrid, Barcelona and Montpellier, and a second between Madrid, Vitoria and Dax. The total investment in Spain in the context of the priority transport project No. 3 amounts to €12,014 million.

Priority transport project No. 8, establishing a multimodal (train and road) link between Portugal – Spain and Central Europe, with a total investment in Spain of €1,696 million.

Spain receives financial support for TEN projects in the context of the Cohesion Fund. The total support between 1993 and 1999 amounted to €4,605.5 million, including €2,609 million for road infrastructure, €1,860.3 million for railways, €28 million for ports, €73.2 million for airports and €35 million for vessel traffic management systems.

4.2.5 United Kingdom

Characteristics	Central Government	Regional Authorities	Local Government
Infrastructure policy as basic tool to support economic development	Construction and maintenance of transport infrastructure in England	*Scottish Parliament:* Primary legislative competency for Scottish road network	Actions based on governmental legislation
Large infrastructure projects financed in public private partnership	Transport Safety measures in the UK	Construction of new railways and railway-service	Local government based on statute
Focus on integrated transport	Cooperation with Department of Transport, Environment and the Regions on the one hand and the devolved administrations on the other hand	*National Assembly for Wales:* Secondary legislative construction and maintenance of railways in Wales	Local planning, local transport infrastructure, detailed planning
Significant influence of environmental aspects on transport infrastructure policy	National agency for the administration of transport infrastructure (Highway Agency, Office of the Rail Regulator, Office of Passenger Rail Franchising)	Competency for further transport infrastructure projects in Wales	Local governments receive state funding for specific tasks in the transport infrastructure planning
Liberalisation and privatisation of the railway sector since the early 1990s		*Northern Ireland Assembly:* Competency for transport infrastructure planning and road services	Development of local transport strategies by the local authorities in Scotland (which are related to and interconnected with major transport infrastructure projects)
		English Regional Development Agencies (RDAs): RDAs support investment in infrastructure in the context of their responsibility of promoting regional	Adoption of local transport plans
			Development of local plans for the policy implementation

Characteristics	Central Government	Regional Authorities	Local Government
		development RDAs contribute to programmes and policies in infrastructure policy *Government Offices for the Regions (GOR):* Coordinative function, participation in policy implementation in England Support of integrated transport systems in England	

TEN priority projects in the UK:

The United Kingdom takes part in the EU Transeuropean Network priority transport projects. In this respect, the following projects need to be mentioned:

Priority transport project No. 2, establishing a High Speed Train connection from Paris via Bruxelles, Köln/Frankfurt and Amsterdam to London, with a total investment in the UK section of €4,718 million.

Priority transport project No. 9, constructing a conventional rail line from Cork, via Dublin, Belfast, Larne to Stranraer, with a total investment in Northern Ireland of €119 million.

Priority transport project No. 13, building a road link between Ireland, the UK and the Benelux countries. The investment located in the UK amounts to €2,089 million.

Priority transport project No. 14, establishing and upgrading the West-Coast Main Line railway connection to a high speed train connection. The total investment allocated to this project amounts to €3,000 million.

4.3 Decentralised States

4.3.1 Denmark

Characteristics	National Government	Regional Level (counties – "amter")	Local Level (municipalities – "kommuner")
Investment in the construction and maintenance of infrastructure in the road- and railway sector is characterised as prerequisite for economic development Remarkable influence of environment aspects in the setting of priorities for public infrastructure and in the planning process of major infrastructure projects	Legislative competency and responsibility for planning the major infrastructure projects comparable to TEN Significant influence of specialised agencies on the national level in the planning process (transport agency, similar body for railway sector), which are in charge of the regulation of specific, transnational aspects Decisions on the participation in TEN projects	Implementation tasks related to transport infrastructure Implementation of environmental tasks related to transport infrastructure Responsibility for road maintenance, 2/3 of the road network under county administration Rather limited scope for setting own policy objectives in transport infrastructure policy	Implementation tasks related to transport infrastructure Implementation of environmental tasks related to transport infrastructure Participation in the road maintenance Rather limited scope for setting own policy objectives in transport infrastructure policy

Denmark takes part in the TEN priority transport project No. 11, which establishes the Oresund fixed road / rail link between Denmark and Sweden. The volume of expenditure for the Oresund fixed link amounts to €2,740 million. Additionally, expenditures for the Danish access to roads of €946 million have been foreseen for the period 1992–1999.

4.3.2 Finland

Characteristics	National Government	Regional Level - Provinces	Local Level
Aim to support east – west connections	Planning and construction of major road and railway infrastructure	Participation in the implementation of these projects	Participation in the implementation of transport infrastructure projects
High value of cross-border cooperation in the framework of the "Nordic Dimension Concept" (developing the northern dimension in the EU, including environmental, energy and transport policy)	Implementation of various trans-national agreements in the field of TEN	Regional Councils especially active in TEN with regard to policy implementation	Detailed regional planning for transport infrastructure projects
		Cooperation between national and regional authorities in the implementation of concrete projects	

Within the framework of the priority transport projects of TEN, Finland takes part in project No. 12, establishing a Nordic triangle multimodal (road and rail) corridor. The share of the Finnish section of the project amounts to €2,670 million for the planning period 1980 to 2010.

4.3.3 The Netherlands

Characteristics	National Government	Regional Level - Provinces	Local Level – Muncipalities
Construction of major infrastructure lines (road and railways) High amount of transport runs through The Netherlands Most major transport infrastructure projects have international impact	Planning, construction and maintenance of major transport infrastructure Main road network (motorways) and railways under national authority	Competency for provincial roads Own tax base for road construction However, provincial roads are normally not covered by TEN	Competency for local roads (normally not covered by TEN)

The Netherlands take part in the priority transport project No. 2, establishing a high speed train connection between Paris, Bruxelles, Köln/Frankfurt, Amsterdam and London. The Dutch section amounts to €3,938 million of the total expenditure. Furthermore, the priority transport project no. 5 establishes a conventional rail and conventional transport line from Rotterdam to Emmerich, with the total investment amounting to €4,094 million.

4.3.4 Sweden

Characteristics	National Government	Regional Level (counties – "län" / county councils – "landsting")	Local Level (municipalities – "kommuner")
National investment programme for sectorial infrastructures (railways, motorways)	Planning and construction of major transport infrastructure projects	Counties (län) have consultation rights in the planning phase	Competency for municipal roads and streets (normally not covered by TEN-projects)
Macro-economic and technical approach to the planning and implementation of transport infrastructure projects	Competency of the national level (government and parliament) covers also detailed planning and spatial planning issues in the context of major transport infrastructure projects	The political opportunities for regional authorities to influence planning of TEN is, however, marginal	Consultation rights in the planning phase
	Clear-cut division between the different transport sectors		Marginal opportunities for local authorities to influence planning of TEN

Sweden took part in the Transeuropean Transport priority project No. 11, which established the Oresund fixed link. The total expenditure for the Oresund link amounts to €2,740 million for the period of 1992–2000, with additional expenditures for Swedish access routes of €472 million for the same period of time. Furthermore, Sweden is part of the priority project No. 12, establishing the Nordic triangle multimodal (road and rail) corridor. The share of the Swedish section in the total investment amounts to €7,400 million.

4.4 Two-Tiered States

4.4.1 Greece

Characteristics	National Government	Intermediary Institutions I – Prefectures	Intermediary Institutions II - Regions	Local Authorities – Municipalities
Transport infrastructure policy aims at supporting economic development	Infrastructure planning, construction and maintenance (legislative power and policy implementation)	-----	-----	Limited consultation rights Marginal influence on policy making in the policy field of TEN

The TEN priority project no. 7 establishes a motorway connection between Patra and Piraeus, Piraeus and Igoumenitsa and Piraeus and Kipi. The total investment allocated to this project amounts to €9,242 million.

The financial support provided by the Cohesion Fund for TEN projects between 1993 and 1999 amounts to €1,534.5 million, including €680.3 million for road construction, €484.4 million for railways, €77.6 million for ports, €259.8 million for airports and €32.4 million for vessel traffic management systems.

4.4.2 Ireland

Characteristics	National Government	Geographic Regions - Provinces	Local Authorities – County Councils (and local authorities grouped around counties or large cities)
Aim to integrate Ireland more closely with the EU

Aim to reduce disadvantages resulting from the peripheral status

Underlying objective to support economic development

Particularly active role of the EU with respect to investment in infrastructure

Transport infrastructure policy has to take account into the specific situation of Ireland as an island | Political and fiscal responsibility for TEN and major transport and railway infrastructure projects lies with the national government

Centralisation is extremely visible in the field of TEN

Legislation and policy implementation located at the national level | The provinces are traditional territorial entities within the Irish system, which have, however, no regional power or policy responsibility within the policy field of TEN | Participation in the decision-making on major infrastructure and TEN-projects via the representation in the bicameral parliament |

Transeuropean Network priority project no.9 is located in Ireland, establishing a conventional rail connection between Cork, Dublin, Belfast, Larne and Stranraer (Scotland). The total investment allocated to the project amounts to €357 million. Furthermore, Ireland takes part in priority project no. 13 establishing a road link between Ireland, the UK and the Benelux. The investment allocated in Ireland in the context of this project totals to €1,540 million.

The Cohesion Fund also provides financial support for TEN projects in Ireland. The total sum between 1993 and 1999 amounted to €748.4 million. The various transport sectors took the following share: road construction €559.5 million, railways €141.7 million, ports €38.5 million, airports €3.2 million and vessel traffic management systems €5.5 million.

4.4.3 Luxembourg

Characteristics	National Government	Local Authorities – Municipalities
Transport infrastructure planning, construction and maintenance Policy closely interrelated with environmental and transport safety issues Aim of close interrelation of national and European transport infrastructure	Legislation on, planning and implementation of major transport infrastructure projects	Consultation rights in the planning phase of concrete projects

Due to the small size of Luxembourg, none of the priority projects for Transeuropean Networks in the current planning period of 2000 to 2006 is located in Luxembourg. However, Luxembourg is benefiting from the positive economic effects resulting from the TEN priority projects located in the neighbouring countries, especially those in Belgium. For the projects in Belgium, France and Germany please see the chapters of the respective countries.

5. *Regional and Structural Policy*

In taking a historical perspective on the policy field it should be mentioned that the political concept inherent in the EU Regional and Structural Policy, namely to contribute to regional and structural development, was already included into the founding treaties of the European Communities. The basic approach to economic development policy was based on the approach that market integration and the removal of trade barriers would lead to a strengthened of economic growth and development. Therefore, Regional and Structural Policy was not a separate policy field with genuine objectives and policy tools. Policies and programmes were based on ex-art. 235 EC (art. 308 EC), with making a reference to the preamble, which includes a general obligation to contribute to a harmonious economic development. The importance of regional development policies rose during the 1970s due to the decline of the world economy and the rising structural difficulties, including rising unemployment and regional disparities, in most Member States. The Regional Development Fund (ERDF) was established in 1976 and since the 1980s, the EC has established complex and differentiated instruments for Regional and Structural Policy, including the three structural funds (European Regional Fund, European Social Fund (ESF) and European Agricultural Fund, Section on Guidance). Since 1993, the Cohesion Fund was added to the community means orientated towards the support of economic development. The Cohesion Fund has been introduced in order to support economic development especially in Spain, Greece, Portugal and Ireland and to prepare those countries for the Economic and Monetary Union. Further resources for Structural Policy measures are provided in the context of the fisheries policy, transport, energy and environmental policy. Since the Single European Act, Regional and Structural Policy has been included in the TEC as separate policy. Regional and Structural Policy gained new momentum and was subject to intensive discussions in the context of the southern enlargement, the agreement on EMU and currently in the context of the eastern enlargement.

Financial resources for the EU Regional and Structural Policy are provided by the structural funds – the European Regional and Development Fund (ERDF), as defined in article 160 EC (ex-art. 130 C), the European Social Fund (ESF) as laid down in art. 146 – 148 EC (ex-art. 123 – ex-art. 125), the European Agricultural Guidance and Guarantee Fund, Guidance Section, as specified in art. 34 EC (ex-art. 40) and the Cohesion Fund (art. 161 EC (ex-art. 130 D)). In the current planning period of 2000 – 2006, the total sum for Regional and Structural Policy in the EU budget amounts to €195 billion, which is the 2nd highest position of the budget.

The ERDF is designed to help to redress the main regional imbalances in the Community through participation in the development and structural adjustment of regions whose development is lagging behind. The EU is also active in the conversion of declining industrial regions.

The Cohesion Fund provides a financial contribution for projects in the fields of environment and Trans-European Networks (transport infrastructure, art. 161 EC). Member States benefiting from the Cohesion Fund are Spain, Greece, Portugal, and Ireland. Currently, 50.3% of the financial means are provided for environmental projects and 49.7% for transport infrastructure projects. Therefore projects financed by the Cohesion Fund clearly indicate the close interrelation of the policy fields of Regional and Structural Policy and TEN.

Turning from the historical development of the policy field to the policy objectives, it needs to be stressed that economic and social cohesion, as laid down in art. 158 – 162 EC (ex-art. 130 A – ex-art. 130 E) is one of the most important policies of the European Community. Art. 158 § 1 EC contains a general clause, which provides for a stronger economic and social cohesion in order to realize a harmonic development of the Community. In order to promote the economic and social cohesion and the harmonious development of the European economies, three specific objectives have been defined for the Community Regional and Structural Policy. These are:

- Objective 1: Providing economic support for regions, whose economic development is lagging behind. The main focus lies on the investment in infrastructure and the encouragement of investment in business economic activity (financial support is provided for this objective by the ERDF, ESF, EAGGF-Guidance, FIFG).
- Objective 2: Supporting economic and social conversion in industrial, rural, urban or fisheries-dependant areas facing structural difficulties (financial means are provided by the ERDF, ESF).
- Objective 3: Modernising systems of training and promoting employment (financial resources are provided by the ESF).

Additionally, the Community has set up four Community Initiatives, which are orientated towards further, specific problems of the economic development. These are:

– Interreg III, covering and promoting cross-border, transnational and interregional cooperation intended to encourage the harmonious, balanced and sustainable development of the whole Community area (financed by the ERDF).
– Urban II aims at supporting the economic and social regeneration of cities and of urban neighbourhoods in crisis with a view to promote a sustainable urban development (financed by the ERDF).
– Leader +, which is designed to support the rural development (financed by EAGGF, Guidance Section).
– Equal contributing to the support of transnational cooperation to promote new means of combating all forms of discrimination and inequalities in connection with the labour market (financed by the ESF).

Of specific importance for the implementation of Regional and Structural Policy is the principle of partnership developed by the European Commission. The principle of partnership is the key to involve regions, not just national governments, in formulating and implementing Regional and Structural Policy. Because EU measures complement corresponding national programmes, there has to be close cooperation and consultation among the Commission, Member States and regional or local bodies at all stages of a structural programme. Eligible Member States' plans for regional assistance are incorporated into Community Support Frameworks – contractual agreements between the Commission and national and regional authorities. Community

Support Frameworks set out the program's priorities, type of aid, methods of financing and further rules for the policy implementation. Moreover, the Commission can take the initiative and propose that Member States or regions participate in operations of particular interest to it. Based on these rules and regulations, the principle of partnership constitutes a cooperation mechanism which does not result from and is not interconnected with the national territorial structure analysed in this study, but which is rooted in EC norms.

Regional and Structural Policy is one of the policy fields, which is very closely interrelated and interconnected with other EU policies. Most importantly, Regional and Structural Policy is designed as an integrated, cross-sectoral policy, which has to be respected in the implementation of various other policy fields. The cross-sectoral clause in the design of the Regional and Structural Policy implies that the effects of other EU policies on the regional economic development have to be considered in the design and implementation of these policies. The cross-sectoral clause of Regional and Structural Policy has the most visible impact on the implementation of the Single Market Policy and Competition Policy. By providing financial support for economically weak regions and sectors, the EU Regional and Structural Policy aims at preparing these for the competition in the Single Market. The efforts of the Member States related to the reduction of unbalanced economic development have to be considered in the implementation of the Single Market Policy. A comparable interrelation exists with regard to the Common Agricultural Policy (CAP), which includes, as explained above, a Structural Policy dimension (guidance section of the European Agricultural Fund). Furthermore, the development of rural areas is an explicit objective of the EU Regional and Structural Policy. A clear separation between rural development in the context of the CAP and

Regional and Structural Policy has hardly been established. Further policies that have implications for and are interrelated with the regional development are Transport Policy and Environmental Policy, which have to take different economic development into consideration. An additional interrelation exists between Regional and Structural Policy and the policy on the establishment of Transeuropean Networks. Transeuropean Networks are co-financed by the Cohesion Fund and are designed to contribute to the economic development. Finally, the intersection of the ESF with labour market and employment policies has to be mentioned. According to art. 146 EC (ex-art. 123), it is the task of the ESF to improve employment opportunities for workers, by improving the employability of workers, by increasing their geographical and occupational mobility, and by facilitating their adaptation to industrial changes and to changes in production systems. With these objectives, the European Social Fund is closely related to and interconnected with the national employment policies and the EU Social Policies (art. 136 EC (ex-art. 117)). As employment policy had already been dealt with in the study on the "Amsterdam Fields of Mandatory Consultation", only the general, central characteristics of national policies are recalled in this study.

Beside these interrelations between policy fields explicitly mentioned in the TEC, a further aspect has to be considered. The EU has recently started to develop a policy on spatial planning, leading to the European Spatial Development Perspective (ESDP). The ESDP aims at contributing to a discussion within the EU Member States and with the EU institutions on the topic of spatial planning. It aims at establishing a joint point of departure and common instruments for spatial planning. The spatial planning policy and conception is very closely interrelated with the EU Regional and Structural

Policies, which can be illustrated by the fact that the ESDP has been based on article 158 EC (ex-art. 130 A), which forms also the general legal basis for actions leading to the strengthening of economic and social cohesion. The conception of the ESDP includes three main objectives:

- The development of a balanced and polycentric urban system and a new urban/rural relationship;
- The securing of parity of access to infrastructure and knowledge;
- The sustainable development, prudent management and protection of nature and the cultural heritage.

The conception, which was decided at an informal meeting of the Council of Ministers, includes policy guidelines for the Member States, regions, local authorities and the European Commission. A specific focus is laid on the development of urban and rural areas, border regions and areas with specific geographic characteristics (mountain regions, coastal regions and islands). The ESDP suggests concrete policy options for each of the three policy objectives. By giving the policy options, the EU Member States aimed at making the ESDP a suitable and operational tool for achieving a sustainable and territorially balanced development. The document is not legally binding, nor does it contain new responsibilities or competencies for the European institutions. The approach taken by the ESDP fully respects the principle of subsidiarity. In an additional, informal meeting of the ministers responsible for spatial planning and urban/regional policy in 1999, an action programme has been launched, which includes the objectives of the ESDP and which is financed by the Structural Funds.

With respect to the evolution of the ESDP and its mentioned interrelations with Regional and Structural Policy, the policy field of spatial planning is included in the tabular overviews on distribution of competencies in the Member States. The approach reflects furthermore the tendency in many Member States of formulating spatial planning policies in close cooperation with Regional and Structural Policy. The interdependence of Regional and Structural Policy and spatial planning is therefore another typical example of the form of horizontal policy making across clearly defined policy fields in the EU. By extending the analysis slightly beyond the legally regulated framework of the EU Regional and Structural Policy, the current report aims at presenting an improved overview on the policies related to regional economic development and cohesion in the EU Member States. Within the EU Regional and Structural Policy, the study lays a focus on the ERDF, the ESF, and the Cohesion Fund, as these are the most relevant policy tools for regional economic development.

As for the other policies, the EU competency and policy approach are limited by a number of factors: Regional and Structural Policy on the EU level is implemented in close cooperation and partnership with the EU Member States. The Community and the Member States are equally in charge of economic policies, which help to attain the objectives as specified in art. 158 EC. EU activities are limited to co-financing, which illustrates that the EU policies aim to complement, rather than replace national policies. According to the general guidelines for Regional and Structural Policy, policy-making and implementation shall be characterised by transparency, partnership and subsidiarity. Therefore, Regional and Structural Policy is a typical example of parallel, complementing activities of the Member States and the EU.

The analysis of the distribution of competencies and the political practice in the Member States in Regional and Structural Policy clearly demonstrate that the policy related to economic and social cohesion is a major field of action for the regional and local level. The regional and local levels fulfil important tasks in this policy field and regional and local authorities are intensively involved in the policy process. The only exceptions to this general rule are the two-tiered states, where the involvement and political influence of the sub-national level is still rather limited and implemented in a top-down approach. Most of the political channels of access for sub-national players in two-tiered states within the policy field of EU Regional and Structural Policy are related to the implementation of the EU principle of partnership. These forms are not constitutionally or legally guaranteed forms of participation within the domestic political system.

The sub-national players have developed a wide range of formalised and informal cooperation and coordination within their national system as well as in relation to the EU-level, which include direct channels of access (for example via the regional offices in Brussels, which are particular active in the field of Regional policy). In the interviews conducted in the context of the study, most regional and local representatives identified the Regional and Structural Policy as the policy field with the strongest effect on the regional and local level and as a major policy field the CoR should concentrate on.

5.1 Federal States

5.1.1 Austria

Characteristics	Federal Government	Regional Government - Länder	Local Government
Policy field of ERDF Increase chances of employment in certain regions Support adaptation of regional economic structures Investment in infrastructure Programme based economic support Spatial planning used for regional development purposes Regional policy mainly orientated towards sectoral support, only to lesser extent regional focus	**Policy field of ERDF** Only basic principles are regulated by legislation Sectoral competencies related to regional economic development, e.g. trade and industry law (*"Gewerberecht"*), Transport legislation, legislation on water and forests National level sets up own economic support programmes Significant political influence on regional economic development due to the limited financial means of the subnational levels	**Policy field of ERDF** Setting of regional political priorities, developing programmes and implementing regional policy Regional economic and infrastructure planning in cooperation with the federal level, implementation of programmes to support regional development is limited by the availability of financial means Participation in the administration of regional policy (*"mittelbare Bundesverwaltung"*) under the responsibility of the Land governor (*"Landeshauptmann"*)	**Policy field of ERDF** Participation in the implementation of Regional and Structural Policy, local implementation of Regional and Structural Policy regulated in the federal constitution Programmes to support the local economy Local economic development concepts and strategies

Characteristics	Federal Government	Regional Government - Länder	Local Government
Spatial Planning	**Spatial Planning**	**Spatial Planning**	**Spatial Planning**
Spatial planning carried out at all three levels	Federal level does not have competency for comprehensive planning, no specific ministry	Competency for comprehensive spatial planning	Local spatial planning
Sectoral planning with territorial reference	Sectoral planning with spatial implications in various ministries	Setting of legal framework for spatial planning	Participation of the local authorities in Länder spatial planning, forms of participation vary between the Länder
Close interrelation of spatial planning, regional policy and regional planning	Coordinating function of the federal chancellery	Implementation of spatial planning programmes as well as sectoral regional plans	Administration of building permits
Significant role of the Austrian Conference for Spatial planning for the policy process, based on a political agreement of all three levels ("Österreichische Raumordnungskonferenz")		Plans form the framework and basis for local activities in spatial planning	Local land use plans ("Flächenwidmungsplan")
		Regulation of the spatial planning instruments	In some Länder, local authorities have set up local development schemes ("Räumliches Entwicklungskonzept"), which fix guidelines for the future development of the municipal territory
		Supervision of activities on municipal level	Building regulation plan ("Bebauungsplan")
			Local spatial planning is one of the autonomous tasks of the municipalities under general state supervision (approval of spatial planning, verification on the conformity with spatial planning laws at the regional and national level)

Characteristics	Federal Government	Regional Government - Länder	Local Government
Policy field of ESF Focus on elderly, women, youth and long-term unemployed Yearly fixed policy objectives for unemployment policy (national action plan) Policy guidelines are in line with the EU policies	**Policy field of ESF** Labour market and employment policy formulated by the national government Formulation of policy objectives, legislation and employment programmes Provision of financial support for local and regional employment programmes National employment service	**Policy field of ESF** Regionalised structure of the labour market services Implementation of measures to support the local labour market	**Policy field of ESF** Constitutional competencies of the local level in labour market policy very limited, more important role in political practice Implementation of measures to support the local labour market by making use of local economic support policy Increased activities of local authorities in employment policies in recent years Setting of positive incentives for labour market

In the current programming period (2000 – 2006) Austria receives total financial support of €1,473 million, including €261 million under objective 1, €578 million under objective 2 and €528 million under objective 3. The remaining €4 million are covered by the Fisheries Instrument.

Under the Community Initiatives, Austria receives €183 million in the framework of Interreg III, €8 million in the framework of Urban II, €96 million in the context of Equal and €71 million in the framework of the Leader+ community initiative[6].

---

[6] The figures on the allocation of financial support under the three objectives of the EU Regional and Structural Policy are taken from: European Commission / DG Regional Policy and Cohesion: Inforegio news, Newsletter No. 65, June 1999 and for the community initiatives: http://www.inforegio.cec.eu.int

5.1.2 Belgium

Characteristics	Federal Government	Regional Government		Local Government
		Regions	Communities	Provinces / Municipalities
Policy field of ERDF	Policy field of ERDF	Policy field of ERDF	-----	Policy field of ERDF
Stimulate and strengthen economic growth	Economic policy matters that affect the Economic and Monetary Union of Belgium	Regional development policy		Local economic development policy in the context of the general competency of local self-administration
Facilitate entrepreneurship		Economic policy in a broad sense		
Regional development plans on the level of the Belgian regions	Fiscal policy	Regional investment companies, subsidy policy		Local economic support
Investment in infrastructure	Trade and company law, intellectual property rights			Management of economic affairs of provincial or municipal importance
Support of small and medium size enterprises	Setting framework for public tenders			
Support programmes for regions and economic sectors				

Characteristics	Federal Government	Regional Government		Local Government
		Regions	Communities	Provinces / Municipalities
Spatial Planning Policy Separate planning systems of the three Belgian regions and the municipalities Development and implementation of regional land use plans ("*Plans de destination*" / "*Bestimmingsplan*")	**Spatial Planning Policy** Spatial Planning has been transferred from the national level to the regional level in the state reforms of 1980 and 1988 No federal competency, no supervisory power on the regional competencies, however, some institutions like the State Council and the Court of Arbitration play a judicial and advisory role in spatial planning policy	**Spatial Planning Policy** Spatial planning is a regionalised competency, no federal supervision Regions determine their spatial planning policy and spatial planning systems Regions establish planning legislation and regulations Regional government issues building permits for major infrastructure projects	--	**Spatial Planning Policy** Development and implementation of local land use plans Municipal destination plans / municipal structure plans Granting of building permits Possibility to organise policy-making and service provision on inter-municipal basis

Characteristics	Federal Government	Regional Government		Local Government
		Regions	Communities	Provinces / Municipalities
Policy field of ESF	Policy field of ESF	Policy field of ESF	----	Policy field of ESF
Aim to reduce long term unemployment and youth unemployment Support of part-time employment	Labour law Social security	Employment support programmes		Support local employment possibilities Management of employment policy measures of provincial or municipal importance

In the current planning period (2000–2006) Belgium receives a total support provided by the structural funds of €1,829 million, including €625 million under objective 2, €737 million under objective 3 and €34 million in the context of the Fisheries instrument. Additional support is provided for former objective 1, 2 and 5 b areas.

Belgium is currently benefiting from the following community initiatives: Interreg III (104 million €), Urban II (20 million €), Equal (€70 million) and Leader+ (€15 million).

5.1.3 Germany

Characteristic	Federal Government	Regional Government - Länder	Local Government
Policy field of ERDF	**Policy field of ERDF**	**Policy field of ERDF**	**Policy field of ERDF**
Regional policy as part of general economic policy / social market economy	Since 1969 participation in the regional economic development in the framework of the joint-action of the federal level and the Länder according to a constitutional procedure ("*Gemeinschaftsaufgabe*")	General Länder competency for legislation and policy implementation on regional and structural policy (art. 30 BL)	Provision of financial support and regional / local economic programmes in the context of the competency for local self administration
Setting and maintaining framework for economic activities		Regional economic development programmes	Support local economy
Principle of equal living conditions	Financial contribution in the context of the support of the regional economic development ("*Gemein-schaftsaufgabe*") of DM 54 billion	Regional support programmes corresponding to the specific needs of the region	Local economic development strategies
Focus on employment promoting investment and investment in infrastructure		Participation in the framework of the joint-action of the federal level and the Länder ("*Gemeinschaftsaufgabe*"): Länder receive 50% of expenditure from the federal level and contribute the other 50% themselves)	Support of start-up programmes
Support of east German Länder, economic transition to market economy, activities of all levels of government			
Financial resources provided by the federal level between 1999–2002 for the new German Länder: support of innovation: DM 3 billion,		Increased dependency of the Länder on the support of the federal level	

Characteristic	Federal Government	Regional Government - Länder	Local Government
support of regional economic structure (*Gemeinschaftsaufgabe*) DM 2 billion, infrastructure DM 67 billion Support of regions affected by structural changes Support by providing subsidies and loans, investment in infrastructure			
Spatial Planning Policy Legal framework for spatial planning is provided by the federal level to ensure certain degree of uniformity Regulation of land use and country planning	**Spatial Planning Policy** Only general regulations are made on the federal level Close cooperation in spatial planning with the Länder, conference on spatial planning of the federal level and the Länder National report on spatial planning issues (not on a strict yearly basis, multi-annual reports)	**Spatial Planning Policy** Responsibility for spatial planning at the level of the Land Länder exercise spatial planning on two levels: state development plan (for the whole Land) and regional plans	**Spatial Planning Policy** Competency for local spatial planning in context of the local self administration Local land use plans Participation of the local authorities in the regional plans

Characteristic	Federal Government	Regional Government - Länder	Local Government
Policy field of ESF	**Policy field of ESF**	**Policy field of ESF**	**Policy field of ESF**
Reduction of long-term unemployment	General legislative power	Implementation of employment policy measures	Take part in the implementation of job-creating measures
Counterbalance effects of East German transition	Provides framework for programmes and job creating measures	Operate as partners in the territorial employment pacts	
Reduction of regional imbalances	Principles for public employment service	Setting up of job-creating measures in cooperation with the federal level	
	Unemployment insurance		

According to the planning document of the period 2000-2006 for the EU Regional and Structural policy, Germany receives €19,229 million under the objective 1 support framework, €2,984 million under the objective 2 and €4,581 million under objective 3. With additional support resulting from the transition support for former objective 1, 2 and 5b areas and the Fisheries instrument, the total support framework amounts to €28,156 million.

In the current framework, Germany is benefiting from the following Community Initiatives: Interreg III (€737 million), Urban II (€140 million), Equal (€484 million), Leader+ (€247 million).

5.2 Regionalised States

5.2.1 France

Characteristics	National Government	Regional Authorities – Régions	Local Authorities – Départements / Communes
Policy field of ERDF	**Policy field of ERDF**	**Policy field of ERDF**	**Policy field of ERDF**
Adaptation of the national regional and structural policy to EU standards and concepts	Definition of national priorities, policy objectives and overall framework for regional development policies	Competency for development and implementation of regional development plans	Complementary local initiatives for supporting economic development
Support of regional economic development	Distribution of EU funding for regional development		
Increased role of the regions since reform of June 1989			
Spatial Planning	**Spatial Planning**	**Spatial Planning**	**Spatial Planning**
Spatial planning includes country, town planning and rural development	Definition of national objectives, policy guidelines and framework for spatial planning policy	Development and definition of regional plans	Départements and Communes participate in the spatial planning of cities, environmental planning and country planning
Close interrelation with regional development policy, special emphasis on spatial planning policies in the context of regional development		Spatial planning of cities in cooperation with the local authorities	Spatial planning in cooperation with regions and within the legal framework and overall
Significant influence of environmental and social policy objectives in the spatial		Environmental and	

Characteristics	National Government	Regional Authorities – Régions	Local Authorities – Départements / Communes
planning process		country planning	objectives of the national government
Policy field of ESF	Policy field of ESF	Policy field of ESF	Policy field of ESF
Shift from social measures to active labour market policies Supply-sided economic policy approach	Employment and labour market policies under political authority of the national government	Regional employment and training programmes Function of Mediation in cooperation with social partners	Implementation of programmes by the prefect in cooperation with the local authorities

In the current programming period for the European Regional and Structural Policy, France receives €3,254 million under the objective 1 framework, €5,437 million under objective 2 and €4,540 million under objective 3. The total volume of support (including transitional support of former support areas and the fisheries instrument) amounts to €14,620 million.

Within the framework of the EU Regional and Structural Policy, France is taking part in the following Community Initiatives: Interreg III (€397 million), Urban II (€96 million), Equal (€301 million) and Leader+ (€252 million).

5.2.2 Italy

Characteristics	National Government	Regional Authorities – Regions	Local Authorities	
			Provinces	Municipalities
Policy field of ERDF Until the 1990s, Regional and Structural Policy of low priority in the national context Since 1990ies programme based Regional Policy, strong link to EU programmes and EU co-financing Growing competition between the regions to receive EU funds	**Policy field of ERDF** In certain, limited cases, organisation and implementation of regional development programmes	**Policy field of ERDF** Tendency towards decentralisation of Regional and Structural Policy Formulation and implementation of Regional and Structural Policy major competency of the regions Programming and planning on the regional level	**Policy field of ERDF** Support of local economic development	**Policy field of ERDF** Urban planning and urban development Business start up programmes Local economic support programmes
Spatial Planning Spatial Planning drawn up and implemented by central and local government Basic planning instrument for the whole country on the national level Both strategic promotion of development and detailed regulation of	**Spatial Planning** Spatial planning concepts are developed by the national government Definition of general, legal planning framework	**Spatial Planning** Spatial planning for the respective region on the basis of the national guidelines Formulation and implementation of regional plans and guideline for local activities in spatial planning,	**Spatial Planning** Planning role for their territory in accordance with national guidelines	**Spatial Planning** Municipalities prepare master planning for their territory Division of territory in different land

Characteristics	National Government	Regional Authorities – Regions	Local Authorities	
			Provinces	*Municipalities*
development and detailed regulation of land use	Setting of guidelines for planning, taking account of the economic planning Regulation of land-use guidelines Guidelines provide incentives and prevent paralysis of land-use planning activities	however no direct obligations for local actions	and regional laws, programmes and plans Local land use plans, infrastructure planning	use zones Implementation of urban planning, detailed planning in accordance with rules set by higher levels of government
Policy field of ESF Aim of reducing North-South gap in employment Investment in human resources Training programmes for re-entry in the labour market	**Policy field of ESF** Competency for legislation and implementation of employment policies Administration of unemployment benefits	**Policy field of ESF** Important tasks in vocational training and enterprise creating policies Administration of public employment services	Policy field of ESF Participation in local actions to support employment	Policy field of ESF Participation in local actions to support employment

In the constitutional reform of March 2001, the competency for spatial planning has been attributed to the regions. The national level sets within the policy field only the general framework and the aspects of national interest. The current reform was subject to the referendum in October 2001 and has been approved by 64.2% of the voters. However, the political consequences of the reform remain to be seen.

In the programming period of 2000 – 2006, Italy receives €21,935 million under the objective 1 support framework, €2,145 million under objective 2 and €3,744 million under objective 3. Adding the support under the phasing out of former programmes and the fisheries instrument, the total support volume amounts to €28,484 million.

Italy receives financial support in the framework of the following community initiatives: Interreg III (€426 million), Urban II (€108 million), Equal (€371 million), Leader+ (€267 million).

5.2.3 Portugal

Characteristics	National Government	Regional Authorities		Local Authorities	
		Autonomous regions	Districts / Regional Boards of National Ministries	Municipalities	Parishes
Policy field of ERDF Open economy, important trade relations with EU countries Start of national regional policy in the 1980s Central aims are support of economic development, reduction of regional imbalances, modernisation of infrastructure Vital importance of the support provided by the Cohesion Fund	Policy field of ERDF Competency for formulation and coordination of Regional Policy Coordination and application of Structural Funds Implementation of measures covered by ERDF	Policy field of ERDF Competency should have been transferred to the regions in the state reform of 1998, reform failed Administrative and implementation tasks fulfilled by Autonomous Regions of Azores and Madeira and of the Regional Boards of National Ministries (for continental Portugal) Azores and Madeira have separate physical planning departments in their regional government		Policy field of ERDF Administration of public goods and properties Support of local development	Policy field of ERDF Participation in the municipal policy making via programming contracts, projects on water supply, maintenance of roads etc.

Characteristics	National Government	Regional Authorities		Local Authorities	
		Autonomous regions	Districts / Regional Boards of National Ministries	Municipalities	Parishes
Spatial Planning Land-use planning Regional and local development plans Urban planning Cross-sectoral implications of spatial planning (agricultural policy, environmental policy, regional and structural policy etc.)	**Spatial Planning** Central spatial planning ministry on the national level Preparation of relevant legislation and policy guidelines Definition of regional and local principles for land-use policies and criteria for spatial organisation	**Spatial Planning** The autonomous regions have separate spatial planning departments The regional governments of Azores and Madeira are competent for regulating aspects of spatial planning for their territory	For continental Portugal, the competency for the implementation of national legislation and policy objectives remains with the districts / regional boards of the national ministers	**Spatial Planning** Preparation of local plans Local land use plans, legally binding administrative regulations Municipal development plans Responsibility for preparing majority of plans lies with the local authorities	----

Characteristics	National Government	Regional Authorities		Local Authorities	
		Autonomous regions	Districts / Regional Boards of National Ministries	Municipalities	Parishes
Policy field of ESF	Policy field of ESF	Policy field of ESF	Policy field of ESF	Policy field of ESF	Policy field of ESF
Lower priority compared to regional economic development Growing employment in recent years, comparatively low unemployment rate (4.7% in 1998)	Formulation of policy objectives and legislation for the corresponding national policies		Districts / regional boards of the national ministers implement the national policy objectives and programmes in the policy field corresponding to the ESF	Local authorities take over administrative and implementation tasks	Local authorities take over administrative and implementation tasks

In the current programming period (2000–2006), Portugal receives €16,124 million under the objective 1 framework and additional support for former objective 1 areas (€2,905 million). Portugal is not covered by the objective 2 and objective 3 support framework. Portugal receives support provided by the Cohesion Fund, taking a share of the total expenditure of the Cohesion Fund of 16% – 18%. The total budget of the Cohesion Fund has been fixed at the level of €18 billion.

Portugal receives financial support in the context of the four community initiatives with a share a volume of €394 million (Interreg III), €18 million (Urban II), €107 million (Equal) and €152 million (Leader+).

5.2.4 Spain

Characteristics	National Government	Regional Authorities – Autonomous Communities (AC)	Local Authorities – Provinces and Municipalities
Policy field of ERDF Constitutional norm of an equal and balanced economic development, constitutional obligation to reduce regional imbalances. Still existing, significant regional differences. Economic activities concentrated in the urban centres. Policy understanding similar to EU context	**Policy field of ERDF** Providing legal and political framework for regional economic policy. National fiscal and economic policy	**Policy field of ERDF** Regional economic development competency of all AC's. Design and implementation of regional development programmes. Active participation in the EU programmes for regional economic development	**Policy field of ERDF** Contribution to the local economy in the context of the general competency for regulating local affairs (local self-administration)
Spatial Planning Process of decentralisation in spatial planning. Central aim is proper use of the territory, aim to contribute to the protection of the country's	**Spatial Planning** General responsibility for spatial planning, provision of legal and political framework for spatial planning policies on the regional and local level	**Spatial Planning** Competency for developing and implementing land planning laws. Competency to plan the territory, regional development, housing and further matters of spatial planning	**Spatial Planning** Obligation to establish, adopt and revise structures of planning and land-use. Local land use planning in accordance with the

Characteristics	National Government	Regional Authorities – Autonomous Communities (AC)	Local Authorities – Provinces and Municipalities
nature and environment Important role of public and private organisations (agents) in the spatial planning process Sustainable development of society, equal distribution of benefits and burdens, obligation to guarantee proper housing to all citizens	Principle of framework control: plans of the lower level must not contradict planning of the higher level Regulations on the national level are mainly restrictive, aim to avoid undesirable development Setting framework and coordination of general planning and economic activity	Responsibility for public works and transport infrastructure if they fall completely within their territory Promotion and planning of tourism within the limits of the AC	principles and regulations set by the AC and the national level Responsibility for building permits and other permits Local land planning committees
Policy field of ESF Close cooperation between national government, AC's and social partners Orientated towards certain groups on the labour market Aim of reducing regional imbalances	**Policy field of ESF** Policy area mainly under authority of the national government; national government sets policy objectives and guidelines Parallel structures for certain areas (e.g. training)	**Policy field of ESF** Provision of resources for training Coordination and implementation of national policies Setting up and running of public employment services	**Policy field of ESF** Implementation of concrete projects in cooperation with the Autonomous Communities and the national government

In the programming period of 2000 to 2006, Spain receives financial support under objective 1 (€37,744 million), objective 2 (€2553 million) and objective 3 (€2,140 million). Further support is provided by transitional support for former support areas and in the context of the fisheries instrument (with the total amount in the context of the structural funds being €43,087 million). The European Communities provide financial support for Spain in the framework of the Cohesion Fund (with Spain taking an annual share of 61% – 63.5% of the total amount of €18 billion for the current planning period).

In the framework of the Community Initiatives, Spain receives €900 million in the context of Interreg III, €106 million in the framework of Urban II, €485 million within the Equal community initiative and €467 million in the context of Leader+.

5.2.5 United Kingdom

Characteristics	Central Government	Regional Authorities	Local authorities
Policy field of ERDF Similar approach as on EU-level Programme-based regional policy Main objective is improvement of conditions for private investment	**Policy field of ERDF** Overall responsibility for planning and administration of regional policy, including the EU Structural Funds Provision of legal framework for Regional and Structural Policy Coordinating function	**Policy field of ERDF** *Scottish Parliament:* Management of regional development programmes Policy implementation Planning and preparation of draft programmes, which are coordinated with the national government *National Assembly for Wales:* Management of Regional and Structural Policy *Northern Ireland Assembly:* Management of Regional and Structural Policy *English Regional Development Agencies (RDAs)* Policy implementation, monitoring and	**Policy field of ERDF** Contributes to local economic development Local activities and programmes derive from statute or national legislation Urban planning, transport infrastructure planning Local economic support programmes

Characteristics	Central Government	Regional Authorities	Local authorities
		administration	
		Responsibility for regional policy in England	
		Government Offices for the Regions (GOR):	
		GOR support private investment in the English regions	
		Provision of financial support programmes for business and employment in England	
		Coordinative function and participation in policy implementation in England	
Spatial Planning	**Spatial Planning**	**Spatial Planning**	**Spatial Planning**
Comprehensive and rigorous system of town and country planning	Supervision and control of the planning systems	*Scottish Parliament*	Local activities and programmes derive from statute or national legislation
Large number of non-departmental public bodies	Formulation and publication of national and region-specific guidance	Legislative competency for spatial planning, considerable autonomy including EU affairs in	Local planning, especially local spatial planning, town and

Characteristics	Central Government	Regional Authorities	Local authorities
taking part in the policy shaping of spatial planning		spatial planning	country planning
Comprehensive regulation of land use and development		Cross-sector approach to spatial planning	Local authorities regulate and formulate local policy instruments
Differentiation and flexibility in the decision-making (national and regional guidance etc.)		*National Assembly of Wales* Responsibility for a large number of areas covered by or related to spatial planning, e.g. agriculture, fishery, housing, water, town and country planning	
No national or regional land use plans, but guidance for regions		Competency for regulating EU affairs related to spatial planning	
		Northern Ireland Competencies for regional policy and spatial planning	
		Regional competency for a large variety of competencies related to spatial planning	

Characteristics	Central Government	Regional Authorities	Local authorities
		Regional Development Agencies (RDAs): RDAs contribute to policies and programmes in the sector of land use policy and spatial planning **Government Offices for the Regions (GOR):** Participation in spatial planning implementation in the English regions Management of spatial planning funding programmes for the English regions	
Policy field of ESF Reduction of regional imbalances Combating youth and long-term unemployment	**Policy field of ESF** Framework legislation on labour market and employment policies National employment regime administered by the national government	**Policy field of ESF** *Scottish Parliament* Economic development and its implications for employment	**Policy field of ESF** Local partnerships for employment and territorial employment pacts

Characteristics	Central Government	Regional Authorities	Local authorities
		National Assembly for Wales Economic development and its implications for employment *Northern Ireland* Economic development and its implications for employment *Government Offices for the Regions (GOR)* Coordinative function for the English regions, participation in policy implementation Management of employment programmes for the English regions	

The UK receives financial support under objective 1 (€5,085 million), objective 2 (€3,989 million) and objective 3 (€4,568 million). Additional support is provided for former support areas, with the total amount of financial support being €15,635 million.

Within the four Community Initiatives, the UK receives €362 million in the context of Interreg III, €117 million in the framework of Urban II, €376 million within the Equal programme and €106 million in the context of Leader+.

5.3 Decentralised States

5.3.1 Denmark

Characteristics	National Government	Regional Level (counties – "amter")	Local Level (municipalities – "kommuner")
Policy field of ERDF	**Policy field of ERDF**	**Policy field of ERDF**	**Policy field of ERDF**
Denmark has terminated its national equivalent to regional policy several years ago	National Ministry for Environment and Energy (Department for Spatial Planning) administers and implements the participation in EU Regional and Structural Policy	Counties are NUTS III level and thus can administer EU-Structural Funds	Beneficiaries of EU Regional Policy
Regional Policy is implemented in the framework of the EU programmes		Beneficiaries of EU Regional and Structural Policy	Negotiate allocation of support through their national associations
Focus on free-market principle		Negotiate allocation of support through their national association	
Entire country in an advanced economic status			
Spatial Planning	**Spatial Planning**	**Spatial Planning**	**Spatial Planning**
Regional and Structural Planning	Spatial planning is shared responsibility of the national government, the county councils and the municipalities	Spatial planning is shared responsibility of the national government, the county councils and the municipalities	Spatial planning is shared responsibility of the national government, the county councils and the municipalities
Land-use regulation	Mandatory national planning reports after	Establish, adopt and revise comprehensive regional structure planning, set up land-	Establish, adopt and revise comprehensive local structure planning, set up land use
Environmental aspects of significant importance in the spatial planning			
Division of the country in urban, recreational and rural zones			

Characteristics	National Government	Regional Level (counties – "amter")	Local Level (municipalities – "kommuner")
	each national election	use regulation	regulation
Planning system is based on framework control, plans of the lower level must not contradict the plans of the higher level Specific objectives of the plans on the different levels vary Regulations established by the planning system are mainly restrictive, system is designed to assure that undesirable developments do not occur	National minister (responsibility of the minister for the Environment) can intervene in the planning process on the local levels	Regional plans with policies, maps and land-use guidelines for the total county area, specification of land-use areas for rural, urban or recreational purposes	Municipal plans with policies, maps and land use regulations for the total municipal area
Policy field of ESF Focus on qualification of people Territorial Employment pacts gained significant importance	**Policy field of ESF** National ministry of Labour and Social Affairs in charge of employment policy Allocation of resources provided by ESF	**Policy field of ESF** Predominant level for the organisation of public employment policy Setting up of labour market councils	**Policy field of ESF** Implementation of specific, employment policy initiatives

Under the current breakdown, Denmark receives financial support from the EU under the objective 2 (€156 million) and objective 3 (€365 million). Additional support is provided under the transitional support for former objective 2 & 5b areas (€27 million) and the Fisheries instrument (€197 million). This support includes the participation of Denmark in the support framework of the four Community Initiatives of Interreg III (€34 million), Urban II (€5 million), Equal (€28 million) and Leader+ (€16 million).

5.3.2 Finland

Characteristics	National Government	Regional Level - Provinces	Local Level
Policy field of ERDF	**Policy field of ERDF**	**Policy field of ERDF**	**Policy field of ERDF**
Policy guidelines and principles set by Regional Development Act	Setting of general policy guidelines, supervisory and coordinating function	Design of programmes for regional development, policy implementation	Participation in the development of regional development programmes
Aim of promoting regional development and a regional balance	Provision of funding for regional development	Certain specific plans, e.g. the regional land-use plans, need to be ratified by the national ministry	
Programme based Regional Policy, geographically determined aid regions		Definition of objectives and strategies for regional development	
National regional policy separate pillar beside the EU programmes			

Characteristics	National Government	Regional Level - Provinces	Local Level
Spatial Planning	**Spatial Planning**	**Spatial Planning**	**Spatial Planning**
Long tradition of spatial planning	National level topics of spatial planning are regulated by the Ministry of the Environment	Mediation between national government and municipalities in spatial planning issues by the provincial state offices (which belong to the state administration)	Exclusive competency for local spatial planning, freedom of municipalities was increased by the reform of spatial planning legislation of 1989/90
Policy guided by international trends for urban planning / urbanism	Regulation of aspects of spatial planning related to environmental protection and environmental policy	Task to protect regional interest, regional-land use plans developed by the regional councils	Municipalities are basic units for local spatial planning and administration
Main spatial planning legislation dates back to the 1950s, reform in 1989/90, which increased freedom of municipalities, increased public participation	National Ministry can set guidelines for specific planning issues of national importance (land use, building, housing, nature protection	Regional plans and programmes are developed in cooperation with the national government and the municipalities	Competency for land-use planning and building issues
	Guidelines for regional planning		Town and building plan
Environmental impact assessment since 1994	Subject related programmes (e.g. shore protection programme)	Active participation in region-specific international and cross-border activities of spatial planning and regional development	Responsibility for local infrastructure
	No national spatial plan, policy orientated towards specific issues		All towns and municipalities have similar obligations, even though there are differences in resources, size and population

Characteristics	National Government	Regional Level - Provinces	Local Level
Policy field of ESF	**Policy field of ESF**	**Policy field of ESF**	**Policy field of ESF**
Reduction of long-term unemployment and youth unemployment	Provision of legislative framework, setting of policy objectives	Establishment of 15 regional unemployment and economic development centres with labour market departments	Emphasis on local partnerships in employment policy
Labour market: Multi-level bargaining structure with tripartite bodies at all levels of government	Provision of unemployment benefits	Support of the economic development and promotion of employment	Local employment offices, often on an inter-municipal basis
	Setting up of institutions for specific employment policy measures		Registration of unemployed job-seekers receiving benefits, practical training, vocational training etc.

In the current planning period, Finland receives €913 million under objective 1 and €459 million under objective 2. Further support is provided under objective 3 (€403 million), in the context of the Fisheries Instrument (€31 million) and under the transitional support for former objective 2 and 5b areas. Additional support is provided by the Community initiatives in the framework of Interreg III (€129 million), Urban II (€5 million), Equal (€68 million) and Leader+ (€52 million).

5.3.3 The Netherlands

Characteristics	National Government	Regional Level – Provinces	Local Level – Municipalities
Policy field of ERDF Long tradition of national regional policy (since first half of 19th century) Support of economic development of weaker regions Support of the industry and transformation of the countryside Programme-based regional policy, orientated towards specific economic problems Main difficulties in certain economic sectors (textile and mining)	**Policy field of ERDF** Development of regional policy programmes, setting of policy guidelines and provision of the legislative framework Policy formulation and administration of the participation in the EU-programmes	**Policy field of ERDF** Large autonomy in the detailed planning of Regional and Structural Policy Implementation of Regional and Structural Policy with considerable regional decision-making power	**Policy field of ERDF** Implementation of the national regional policy programmes Comparatively large autonomy in the detailed planning and implementation of Regional and Structural Policy in cooperation with the provinces
Spatial Planning High degree of public regulation with respect to those activities which change spatial environment	**Spatial Planning** Regulation of legal framework for spatial planning Setting overall framework for spatial planning of the whole	**Spatial Planning** Responsibility for regional plans Regional plans are developed for areas larger than the	**Spatial Planning** Local spatial planning, large autonomy of the municipalities in spatial planning matters Municipal planning shall reflect

Characteristics	National Government	Regional Level – Provinces	Local Level – Municipalities
Urban and spatial development regulated by using other policies (e.g. building regulations, provision of infrastructure) Spatial planning is regulated by public intervention Close interrelation of spatial planning with other policies (horizontal coordination, e.g. link to housing policy, stimulation of economic growth, environmental policy, transport)	country in various policy fields Coordination of spatial planning issues between municipalities, provinces and the national government (formal and informal)	municipalities Underlying approach, that larger entities are more suitable for spatial planning issues (e.g. infrastructure projects) Coordination of spatial planning issues between municipalities, provinces and the national government (formal and informal)	the overall planning objectives set by the higher levels Coordination of spatial planning issues between municipalities, provinces and the national government (formal and informal)
Policy field of ESF Reduction of long-term unemployment Improvement of possibilities for employment Qualification and training	**Policy field of ESF** Responsibility for general employment and labour market policy Setting of legal framework for economic development and employment Assure optimal conditions for	**Policy field of ESF** Running of regional employment services	**Policy field of ESF** Decentralised tasks of the administration of unemployment benefits and public assistance Running of employment services

Characteristics	National Government	Regional Level – Provinces	Local Level – Municipalities
	the access to the labour market		
	Administration of labour market services, training and retraining		
	Regulation and administration of unemployment benefits		

Currently, the Netherlands does not receive support under the new objective 1, however under the transitional support for former objective 1 areas (€123 million). Additionally, The Netherlands takes part in the objective 2 (€676 million) and objective 3 (€1,686 million) framework. Further resources are provided by the transitional support for former objective 2 and 5b areas (€119 million) and in the context of the Fisheries instrument (€31 million), with the total sum of support in the context of the Structural Funds amounting to €2,635 million.

In the framework of the Community Initiatives, The Netherlands takes part in the following programmes: Interreg III (€349 million), Urban II (€28 million), Equal (€196 million) and Leader+ (€78 million).

5.3.4 Sweden

Characteristics	National Government	Regional Level (counties – "län" / county councils – "landsting")	Local Level (municipalities – "kommuner")
Policy field of ERDF	**Policy field of ERDF**	**Policy field of ERDF**	**Policy field of ERDF**
Significant EU-influence and process of Europeanisation Process of identifying the region as suitable level for regional policy Support of ultra-peripheral regions Significant interrelation and intersection between national and EU policies	Setting of the overall policy framework and general guidelines for the policy 2 national agencies took over important tasks in the policy implementation	Regional and Structural Policy implementation is a task of the county administrative boards, for the four experimental regions, the competency has been transferred from the state administrative boards to these regions County administrative boards (respectively experimental regions) are in charge of the management of the implementation of EU Structural Funds measures in their region County administrative boards / experimental regions are in charge of regional growth agreements, these are a step towards decentralisation (regional growth agreements determine allocation of funds)	No formal competencies, but the local level is increasingly involved in economic development policies in the political practice

Characteristics	National Government	Regional Level (counties – "län" / county councils – "landsting")	Local Level (municipalities – "kommuner")
Spatial Planning Basis for modern spatial planning in the early urban legislation of the 18th century Since 1947 increasing public power and control on spatial planning issues Aim to stimulate a suitable use and good management of the available land resources, respecting environmental criteria Interrelation of spatial planning and regional development policies	**Spatial Planning** Legal framework and policy guidelines for spatial planning Spatial planning policy under the authority of the Ministry for the Environment and several executive agencies Definition of central, national objectives, which have to be respected in planning of the lower levels	**Spatial Planning** County administrative boards are responsible for spatial planning issues of economic development policy (e.g. definition of industrial areas) County administrative boards are in charge of regional planning (including regional strategies and programmes), county councils in charge of planning in the medical sector and to some extent for regional public traffic County Councils are responsible for planning of regional public traffic services (partly) Overall, the position of the regional level in spatial planning is comparatively weak	**Spatial Planning** Detailed, local spatial planning Significant / important position of the municipalities in the spatial planning process Main focus in spatial planning lies on the municipal level Decisions on local spatial planning, every municipality prepares a comprehensive plan on spatial planning topics (land use, possible areas for development, building permits) Municipal plans are not legally binding, plans are drawn up in consultation

Characteristics	National Government	Regional Level (counties – "län" / county councils – "landsting")	Local Level (municipalities – "kommuner")
			with county administrative boards
Policy field of ESF	**Policy field of ESF**	**Policy field of ESF**	**Policy field of ESF**
Long tradition of national employment policy programmes	Political responsibility for employment and labour market policies	Setting up of county labour market boards	Implementation of local labour market projects
Focus on training and training on the job	Administration of unemployment benefits	County administrative boards in charge of the coordination of the policy implementation with respect to national policy guidelines, measures and programmes	Local commissions dealing with employment issues
			Programmes against youth unemployment
		ESF programmes are worked out in partnership with local authorities, the ESF Council serves as umbrella organisation	Local representative approved as national representative for Sweden in the ESF committee

In the current planning period for the Structural Funds, Sweden receives €722 million under objective 1, additionally €354 million under objective 2 and €720 million under objective 3. Further support is provided in the context of the phasing out of former support areas and by the Fisheries Instrument, with the total sum of support in the context of the Structural Funds amounting to €1,908 million.

Additional support is provided in the framework of the Community Initiatives: Interreg III (€154 million), Urban II (€5 million), Equal (€81 million) and Leader+ (€38 million).

5.4 Two-Tiered States

5.4.1 Greece

Characteristics	National Government	Intermediary Institutions – Prefectures	Intermediary Institutions Regions	Local Authorities – Municipalities
Policy field of the ERDF Similar approach as in the EU context	Policy field of ERDF Policy making, setting political priorities Development of regional development plans	Policy field of ERDF Prefectures support the economic and social development of their area Implementation of regional development projects Prefectural development programmes for national regional policy	Policy field of ERDF Regional Councils suggest projects to be included in support framework Decision is taken by 'Observance Committees' (consisting of regional and state representatives) Marginalisation of the regions in the policy implementation may change in the context of the implementation of the recent reform legislation (1997)	Policy field of ERDF Participation in the implementation of regional and structural policy measures

Characteristics	National Government	Intermediary Institutions – Prefectures	Intermediary Institutions Regions	Local Authorities – Municipalities
Spatial Planning	**Spatial Planning**	**Spatial Planning**	**Spatial Planning**	**Spatial Planning**
General building regulation as major influence on the development of spatial planning	Setting of legal framework, policy objectives and guidelines for spatial planning, regulation of production, approval and implementation of urban plans	Competencies of the national ministries are delegated, within certain limits to the prefectures Spatial plans on the regional level	Regional economic development in close cooperation with prefectures and the national government Implementation of national plans	General urban plan produced for each municipality in accordance with the norms and principles of the national level In general only advisory role of the local authorities with respect to building permits, however a number of municipalities have been empowered to grant building permits
Main instrument are planning studies				
Detailed local planning ratified by governmental decree	National ministry formulates, approves and implements urban plans		Regional plans prepared by the regional authorities according to the guidelines and under the administrative control of the national level	
Regulatory plan provides strategic guidance for large cities				
Complex network of spatial planning procedures and institutions	Management and administration of the system of building control, control of regional plans and regional development policies			
Spatial planning not integrated policy taking account of related policy	Competency shared between Ministry of			

Characteristics	National Government	Intermediary Institutions – Prefectures	Intermediary Institutions Regions	Local Authorities – Municipalities
field (town planning, environmental policy), low degree of policy coordination and intersection	Spatial Planning, Environment and Public Works and other ministries			
Policy field of ESF National employment policy activities corresponding to ESF were subordinate to the principle of monetary stability	**Policy field of ESF** Predominant level for policy formulation and setting of policy objectives Setting up of National Action plans for Employment and involvement of Greece in ESF Regulation and administration of the system of unemployment benefits	**Policy field of ESF** Establishment of Employment Promotion Centres	----	**Policy field of ESF** Participation in the implementation of labour market policies in a rather top-down approach

241

Within the framework of the 3 objectives of the Structural Funds, the financial support for Greece is currently concentrated on objective 1 (€20,961 million). In the framework of the Cohesion Fund, Greece receives 16% – 18% of the total support (of €18 billion) provided by the fund.

In the context of the community initiatives, Greece receives €568 million in the context of Interreg III, €24 million in the framework of Urban II, €98 million within the Equal programmes and €172 million in the context of Leader+.

5.4.2 Ireland

Characteristics	National Government	Geographic Regions - Provinces	Local Authorities – County Councils (and local authorities grouped around counties or large cities)
Policy field of ERDF Similar understanding of Regional and Structural Policy in Ireland compared to the EU Centralised system of policy-making Regional participation originating from EU rules Close link to transport and infrastructure policy Infrastructure investment is integrated into Regional and Structural Policy (e.g. by financial support of the Cohesion Fund) Specific importance of the financial support provided by the Cohesion Fund	**Policy field of ERDF** Regional and Structural Policy formulation and implementation by the national government Formulation of policy guidelines, major priorities, programmes and policy implementation by the national government	**Policy field of ERDF** Verification and implementation of concrete EU Regional Policy measures in cooperation with the national government	**Policy field of ERDF** Participation in the EU Regional and Structural Policy via the EU rules and procedures and the principle of partnership

Characteristics	National Government	Geographic Regions - Provinces	Local Authorities – County Councils (and local authorities grouped around counties or large cities)
Spatial Planning Spatial planning within the Department for Environment No significant planning levels above the local government National agencies are in charge of control tasks No national land-use strategy, however, country-wide planning system **Spatial Planning** National Development Plan developed and designed for the participation in EU programmes Legal right of third parties to appeal planning decisions	**Spatial Planning** Ministry for Environment determines the policy framework in cooperation with the planning appeal boards Delegation of most significant powers to the local planning authorities National ministry has no direct input into development-plan making process or the individual applications	-----	**Spatial Planning** Physical planning and land use policy primary local government activity Making of land-use plans Development plans are most important planning instrument

Characteristics	National Government	Geographic Regions - Provinces	Local Authorities – County Councils (and local authorities grouped around counties or large cities)
Policy field of ESF ESF is an important aspect of the national employment policy Specific focus on training Convergence of national policies to EU approach	**Policy field of ESF** Policy formulation and implementation in the policy field related to the ESF by the national government Formulation of policy guidelines, major priorities, programmes and policy implementation by the national government	**Policy field of ESF** Verification and implementation of concrete EU Regional Policy measures in cooperation with the national government	**Policy field of ESF** Participation in the ESF via the EU rules and procedures

Ireland currently receives financial support in the framework of the Structural Funds under objective 1 (€1,315 million) and in the framework of transitional support for former objective 1 areas (€1,773 million). Ireland receives financial support provided by the Cohesion Fund, with an annual share of 2% – 6% of the total Cohesion Fund expenditure (with the total budget of the Cohesion Fund being €18 billion). Further support is provided by the four Community Initiatives: Interreg III (€84 million), Urban II (€5 million), Equal (€32 million), Leader+ (€45 million).

5.4.3 Luxembourg

Characteristics	National Government	Local Authorities – Municipalities
Policy field of ERDF Focus on support of new technology and investment Assistance to small and medium size enterprises Investment in infrastructure Convergence to EU understanding, Regional policy objectives and programme structure are similar to EU level	**Policy field of ERDF** Legislative and executive competency for regional economic development programmes National Committee for Economic Development Cooperation with the local authorities in the implementation of regional policy programmes	**Policy field of ERDF** Implementation of regional development programmes in cooperation with the national government
Spatial Planning General Spatial Planning including town and country planning Close interrelation of Spatial Planning and regional development policies	**Spatial Planning** National Ministry for Agriculture, Viniculture and Spatial Planning determines main policy objectives National government and parliament determine legal framework for spatial planning policies	**Spatial Planning** Participation in the detailed planning, town and city planning Urban development

Characteristics	National Government	Local Authorities – Municipalities
Policy field of ESF Interrelation of the Luxembourg labour market with the neighbouring countries Support of investment with positive employment effects Policy of wage restraint	**Policy field of ESF** National Ministry of Labour and Employment is responsible for the formulation and implementation of the respective policies Administration of labour market services and unemployment benefits Setting the framework for training and retraining	**Policy field of ESF** Participation in employment promoting measures Participation in local partnerships for employment Running of labour market services Financing of measures to support employment and employability

In the current planning period (2000 – 2006), Luxembourg receives €34 million under objective 2 and €38 million under objective 3. Further, transitional support is provided for former 2 and 5b areas (€6 million). Luxembourg is benefiting from 3 Community Initiatives, namely Interreg (€7 million), Equal (€4 million) and Leader+ (€2 million).

V. Conclusions as regards Committee of the Regions' future work

1. Empirical Findings and Conclusions on the "Maastricht Fields" of Mandatory Consultation

Whereas the first research project on the fields of mandatory consultation of the Committee of the Regions dealt with the policy fields of Social Policy, Employment Policy, Vocational Training, Environmental Policy and Transport Policy, "those policy fields that where newly foreseen for mandatory consultation after the Treaty of Amsterdam", this project has dealt with the fields of mandatory consultation since Maastricht, which are General Training and Youth, Cultural Policy, Public Health, Transeuropean Networks and Regional and Structural Policy. The empirical findings and the recommendations given by the research team are similar for both research projects.

As already stated in the first study, the political context in the Member States within the policy fields of mandatory consultation varies considerably. This variation applies to the understanding and scope, the specific characteristics of the policy field, the distribution of competencies and the shared responsibility of the different levels of government. It applies also for the forms of cooperation and coordination, the channels of political access and the influence in the political practice (as analysed in chapter III of this study).

The form and degree of taking part in the policy-making process as well as the freedom of setting own priorities vary both with respect to the different categories of states (federal states, regionalised states, decentralised states and two-tiered states) and with respect to the different policy fields analysed. It has already been emphasized in the introductory chapters of the five policy fields, that the role of the sub-national level is significantly stronger in the policy fields of Regional and Structural Policy, Cultural Policy and General Training and Youth, compared to the two other policy fields of Public Health and Transeuropean Networks. For Public Health Policy, there is obviously a strong political priority for uniform standards, a uniform policy orientation and a similar policy shaping within the Member States, which leads to a strong position of the national government and national governmental institutions (agencies, public associations etc.) in this policy area. For Transeuropean Networks the resources for planning and financing these major infrastructure projects go beyond the capacity of the regional and local level. This classification does, however, not imply that the regions are not active or do not have a specific interest in these policy fields. The regions are consulted and take part in the planning process of TEN and take an important share in the policy implementation of Transeuropean Networks and Public Health Policy. Furthermore, several representatives from regional offices expressed a strong priority for Transeuropean Networks on the political agenda of their respective region. They underlined, that the projects of Transeuropean Networks are an essential factor and a top priority on the agenda for the economic development of the regions, especially for the more peripheral regions.

Furthermore, as for the first research project, it is important to stress the aspect of joint-policy making in a multi-level framework as concerns these policy fields. This general characteristic has been discussed extensively in the scientific literature in recent years (see for example the concept of multi-level governance developed by Gary Marks, Marks (1996)). The regions take part in the policy-making process, on the one hand by being consulted and by informal channels of access in almost all Member States, one the other hand by taking part in the decision-making via different forms of cooperation, especially in the federal states. In most EU Member States, the patterns of cooperation between the national level and the regional or local authorities are similar for all policy fields, especially as far as the participation of the regions in the preparation of positions for actions at the EU level are concerned. Especially in federal states and to a lesser extent in regionalised states, the regions have a significant freedom for setting own priorities and policy objectives, a characteristic which applies mainly for General Training and Youth, Cultural Policy and Regional and Structural Policy.

Central Empirical Findings and Conclusions on the Fields of Mandatory Consultation:

1. The Regions within the EU and the Committee of the Regions should take specific account of the multi-level character and the high importance of the interrelation between the different levels within the policy fields discussed. The multi-level character applies both to the policy-making in most Member States and for the policy process in the European Union. This multi-level character serves as point of departure for the following recommendations.

2. The political responsibility and the degree of shared or exclusive competencies of the subnational players vary considerably between the 15 EU Member States. As a consequence it may be difficult to agree on priorities. Therefore, the CoR has to take account of these different national traditions and policy patterns.

3. Within the policy fields discussed in this study as well as for the areas covered by the first study on the "Amsterdam Fields of Mandatory Consultation", the pattern of joint-decision making of the different national levels in the Member States is a central characteristic in the preparation of positions at EU level. Policy-making of the regional and local authorities is less characterised by independent policy-making, but by the coordination of policy objectives and priorities and the cooperation between the different levels.

2. Strategic Priorities and Recommendations for the Committee of the Regions

It has already been emphasized in the previous section that the share of the sub-national level in political practice in the five policy fields analysed varies considerably. The distribution of competencies and political responsibility is, however, apparently not a major criterion for setting political priorities. On the one hand, the Committee of the Regions can be an important channel for influencing a policy field at EU level for which no or only weak participation rights are provided for in the national context of the political systems of the EU Member States. A typical example for such a policy field, which strongly affects the regional and local level, in which the regions have a strong political interest, but only limited or marginal participation rights in most Member States, is the policy field of Transeuropean Networks. Several members of regional representations expressed the view that the Committee of the Regions should give strategic priority to the policy field of TEN and that the European policy on Transeuropean Network strongly affects the regional and local level. Compared with the distribution of competencies, two other criteria seem to be more relevant for determining the strategic priorities for the Committee of the Regions. This is especially the aspect of the financial resources allocated to a certain policy field and the financial benefit of a specific community policy, which regional and local entities can expect. Almost all interview-partners of regional offices in Brussels expressed a strategic priority for Regional and Structural Policy; in addition several interlocutors emphasized the preference for the policy field of Transeuropean Networks. In view of the representatives of regional and local entities in

Brussels, the other policy fields, General Training and Youth, Cultural Policy and Public Health are of a significantly lower priority for their activities in Brussels. Nevertheless, education in the European context (i.e. General Training and Vocational Training) remains to be of significance for subnational authorities, as we stated already in the context of the study on the "Fields of Mandatory Consultation since Amsterdam". It is true that competencies in the field of General and Vocational Training are rather limited for the EU, but it has to be stated that in the perspective of cross level policy making and a better problem solving capacity of regional and local authorities, General and Vocational Training seems to be of outstanding importance. It is and it will remain an important task to develop human resources. Since a knowledge-based society in an international context becomes more and more an important factor regarding economic success, it would not be convenient, if the Committee of the Regions would neglect a policy field, from which the regions and local authorities are directly affected and to which they can contribute substantial knowledge and expertise.

A second, important criterion for determining strategic priorities, is the aspect, and this refers also to the last paragraph, if and to which degree a certain policy affects the regional level. Many members of regional offices expressed the priority for concentrating in the work of the Committee of the Regions on core issues and on areas that have a strong impact on the local and regional level. With the concentration on a limited number of areas and issues and the reduction of the number of opinions published, it might be possible to exert a stronger political pressure and to follow up these policy areas more closely. If the aim of influencing European policy-making is a major objective of the Committee of the Regions, the CoR should put more emphasis on elaborating and using its channels of political access.

Besides the fields of mandatory consultation discussed and analysed in this study, the Committee of the Regions should focus on institutional affairs and the institutional development of the European Union. With the institutional reforms introduced by the Treaties of Amsterdam and Nice, the European Union tries to prepare itself for the forthcoming enlargement. However, the challenge inherent in the current enlargement process requires a continuing process of institutional adaptation and reform. The discussions on institutional affairs related to the "Post-Nice Process" are already a significant indication of the relevance of institutional questions in the political debate of the forthcoming years. This includes close follow-up of and participation in the discussions on European Governance and the consultative process related to the White Paper published by the European Commission in July 2001.

> *Recommendations on Strategic Priorities for the Committee of the Regions:*
>
> 1. A stronger focus of activities and opinions on those areas where the regions have both a specific interest and which strongly affect the regional level seems to be useful and necessary. This approach should include a closer follow up of these issues.
>
> 2. Within the five policy fields discussed in this research project, the Committee of the Regions should focus on regional and Structural policy and Transeuropean Networks are the policy fields.
>
> 3. A further strategic priority for the CoR should be the institutional development and the institutional design of an enlarged EU, including the discussions on European Governance.

3. Proposals for Institutional Reforms

Besides the new form of governance in an interdependent multi-level governance framework and the strategic priorities in terms of policy fields, the research team suggests some institutional and procedural reforms in order to strengthen the political role of the Committee of the Regions in the institutional framework of the European Union. The following areas are of specific interest in the context of institutional and procedural reforms, which will be presented in the following.

On a general level, it would be useful and beneficial for the Committee of the Regions to achieve the legal status of a EU organ including the right to apply directly to the European Court of Justice. The institutional status would, furthermore, facilitate inter-institutional cooperation with the Commission and the European Parliament. Inter-institutional cooperation has to be seen as an essential element of exercising political influence and pressure in the EU. With the official status as a EU organ, a more equal partnership of the Committee of the Regions and other EU players might be achieved.

Especially in the context of the forthcoming enlargement, it is of an essential importance to spend greater attention on more research and considerations on an adequate representation of the various regions in the EU. As the membership of all regions in the Committee of the Regions would result in a major problem of size, and the Treaty limits the number of members, new models of representation should be considered. In this respect, the deputy membership in the CoR could be an important channel and pragmatic way of access for these regions to the CoR. Furthermore, rotation systems of membership might be a concept to be considered in a long-term perspective.

In order to increase the political influence of the Committee of the Regions, a more proactive approach could be an essential element. The political statements and opinions of the CoR are often expressed at a too late stage of the political process, where major elements and priorities for a specific proposal are already agreed between the other EU players. In this context, an increased effort on pro-active lobbying might be a useful tool beside general, institutional reforms, which would bring in the opinion of the CoR at an earlier stage.

Finally, the working structures of the CoR need to be streamlined and strengthened. This reform of the internal structures of the CoR should concentrate on an increased role of the commissions and the rapporteur in the commissions. Furthermore, it should be considered to open the commissions for the inputs from national experts and to introduce a procedure for adopting opinions without discussion. In order to streamline the organisational structure of the CoR, a reduction of the size of the Bureau is an important element to be considered.

Recommendations on Institutional Reforms of the Committee of the Regions:

1. The legal status of the CoR as an EU institution, as previously demanded by the CoR in the past, should be achieved.

2. All regions should be represented in the CoR. Without increasing the total number of CoR members, this could be achieved through a corresponding use of the instrument of deputy membership.

3. It is necessary to improve the pro-active approach to policy-making. Opinions should be expressed at an earlier stage and the CoR should put more effort into pro-active lobbying.

4. Successful political performance depends on the administrative resources available. This has to be taken into consideration when adapting internal structures in the context of the enlargement process and in the setting of political priorities.

4. Political Assessment of the Concept of Mandatory Consultation Rights for the Committee of the Regions

The establishment of the Committee of the Regions by the Treaty of Maastricht and the extension of the Fields of Mandatory Consultation by the Treaty of Amsterdam was an important and necessary step towards the institutionalised participation of the sub-national levels of the European Member States in decision-making in the EU. The Committee of the Regions has evolved into an important channel of access especially for those regions being represented in the Committee of the Regions and having only limited alternative channels of access. Federal States like Belgium and Germany use the Committee of the Regions as one of the various levels and channels of influencing European policy making, beside the participation in the Council of Ministers, the interest representation via the regional offices and other formal and informal channels of access. Within this multi-level governance policy pattern, the Committee of the Regions has evolved into an important and institutionalised channel of access.

The 10 Fields of Mandatory Consultation foreseen by the Treaties of Maastricht and Amsterdam cover important areas of regional and local interest and serve as platform for institutionalised, joint interest representation of the regional and local level. A further extension of the mandatory consultation is, however, neither favoured by most of the regional offices consulted in the context of the research project, nor useful from a political point of view. Instead, the research team proposes to concentrate efforts on the existing fields of mandatory consultation and the discussion on institutional reforms of the CoR in the context of the forthcoming enlargement. This approach would allow a closer follow-up of the policy fields. As explained above, a limitation of the scope of activities and a concentration on core areas promise several political and procedural advantages for the future work of the Committee of the Regions. If important legislative or political proposals from the Commission are presented in other areas, which have a strong impact on the regional and local level, the possibility for giving an opinion outside the framework of the mandatory consultation remains open as a further channel of political access.

In this context and summing up the aspect discussed above, a major priority should be given to the overall integration and interrelation of the activities and work programme of the Committee of the Regions into the multi-level-governance network already existing in the EU.

VI. Bibliography

General Information

Arnold, Richard, *Ausschuss der Regionen (AdR) der Europäischen Union, Präsentation im Rahmen des 5. Deutsch-Französischen Kolloquiums der Hochschule Speyer,* July 1998.

Badiello, Lorenza, 'Regional Offices in Brussels: Lobbying from the Inside' in Claeys, Paul-H. et al., (eds.), *Lobbying, Pluralism, and European Integration*, Bruxelles, 1998, pp. 328-344.

Bergsmann, Stefan, 'Die österreichischen Bundesländer und ihre auswärtigen Beziehungen, speziell in der Europäischen Union', in: Raimund Krämer (ed.): *Regionen in der Europäischen Union*, Berlin, 1998, pp.180-203.

Bullmann, Udo, Goldsmith, Michael, and Page, Edward C., 'Regieren unter dem Zentralstaat: Regionen, Kommunen und eine sich verändernde Machtbalance in Europa' in Bullmann, Udo and Heinze, Rolf G. (Hrsg.), *Regionale Modernisierungspolitik. Nationale und internationale Perspektiven*, Opladen, 1997, pp. 109-141.

Bullmann, Udo and Heinze, Rolf G. (Hrsg.), *Regionale Modernisierungspolitik. Nationale und internationale Perspektiven*, Opladen.

Calliess, Christian and Ruffert, Matthias (Hrsg.): *Kommentar zu EU-Vertrag und EG-Vertrag*, Neuwied : Luchterhand, 1999.

Christiansen, Thomas, 'Second Thoughts on Europe's "Third Level": The European Union's Committee of the Regions', in: *Publius: The Journal of Federalism* 26:1,1996, pp. 93-116.

Claeys, Paul-H.,Gobin, Corinne, Smets, Isabelle andWinand, Pascaline (eds.), *Lobbying, Pluralism, and European Integration*, Bruxelles, 1998.

Committee of the Regions, *Regional and Local Government in the European Union*, Brussels.QG-36-01-176-EN-C, 1996.

Conceição-Heldt, Eugénia da, *Dezentralisierungstendenzen in westeuropäischen Ländern. Territorialreformen Belgiens, Spanien und Italiens im Vergleich*, Berlin, 1998.

Engel, Christian, *Regionen in der EG. Rechtliche Vielfalt und integrationspolitische Rollensuche*, Bonn, 1993.

Fernández, Francisco Querol, 'Die Präsenz der spanischen Autonomen Gemeinschaften in Brüssel: das Büro der Regierung von Aragón in Brüssel' in Nitschke, Peter (ed.), *Die Europäische Union der Regionen. Subpolity und Politiken der Dritten Ebene*, Opladen, 1999, pp. 61-72.

Fischer, Thomas and Schley, Nicole, *Europa föderal organisieren: Ein neues Kompetenz- und Vertragsgeüge für die Europäische Union*, Bonn: Europa Union Verlag, 1999.

Hasselbach, Kai, *Der Ausschuss der Regionen in der Europäischen Union: die Institutionalisierung der Regionalbeteiligung in der Europäischen Union unter besonderer Berücksicherung der regionalen und dezentralen Verwaltungsstrukturen in den EU-Mitgliedstaaten,* Köln: Heymann, 1996.

Heichlinger, Alexander, *A Regional Representation in Brussels: The Right Idea for Influencing EU Policy-Making?,* European Institute of Public Administration, Maastricht, 1999.

Hooghe, Liesbeth (ed.), *Cohesion Policy and European Integration. Building Multi-Level Governance,* Oxford, 1996.

Hooghe, Liesbeth and Gary Marks, '„Europe with the Regions": Channels of Regional Representation in the European Union' in *Publius, The Journal of Federalism* 26:1 (Winter), 1996, pp. 73-91.

Hrbek, Rudolf, 'Der Ausschuß der Regionen - Eine Zwischenbilanz zur Entwicklung der jüngsten EU-Institution und ihrer Arbeit', in: Europäisches Zentrum für Föderalismus-Forschung Tübingen (ed.), *Jahrbuch des Föderalismus 2000: Föderalismus, Subsidiarität und Regionen in Europa,* Baden-Baden, 2000, pp. 461-478.

Ismayr, Wolfgang (Hrsg.), *Die politischen Systeme Westeuropas,* Opladen, 1997.

Jeffery, Charlie, 'Regional Information Offices in Brussels and Multi-Level Governance in the EU: A UK-German Comparison', in: *Regional & Federal Studies* 2/96, 1996, pp. 183-203.

Keating, Michael, *The New Regionalism in Western Europe: Territorial Restructuring and Political Change*, Cheltenham, Northampton, 1998.

Lebessis, Notis and Paterson, John, *Evolution in Governance: What Lessons for the Commission? A First Assessment*, European Commission, Forward Studies Unit, Working Paper, 1997.

Le Galès, Patrick, 'Conclusion – government and governance in regions. Structural weaknesses and new mobilisations', in: Le Galès, Patrick and Lequesne, Christian (ed.), *Regions in Europe*, London/New York: Routledge, 1998, pp. 239-267.

Le Galès, Patrick and Lequesne, Christian (ed.), *Regions in Europe*, London/New York: Routledge, 1998.

Loughlin, John, 'Representing Regions in Europe: The Committee of the Regions' in *Regional & Federal Studies* 2/96, 1996, pp. 147-165.

Marks, Gary, Hooghe, Liesbet and Blank, Kermit, 'European Integration from the 1980s: State-Centric vs. Multi-level Governance' in *Journal of Common Market Studies*, vol. 34, No. 3, 1996, pp. 341-378.

McAteer, Mark and Mitchell, Duncan, 'Peripheral Lobbying! The Territorial Dimension of Euro Lobbying by Scottish and Welsh Sub-Central Government' in *Regional & Federal Studies*, N°3, 1996, pp. 1-27.

Mietzsch, Oliver, 'Institutionalisierte Interessenvertretung der Regionen und Kommunen in der EU – Eine Bilanz des Ausschusses der Regionen' in *Aus Politik und Zeitgeschichte* B 25-26, 1998, pp. 34-39.

Nitschke, Peter, *Die Europäische Union der Regionen. Subpolity und Politiken der Dritten Ebene,* Opladen, 1999.

Schwarze, Jürgen (Hrsg.), *EU-Kommentar,* Baden-Baden, 2000.

Smets, Isabelle, 'Les régions se mobilisent - quel "lobby régional" à Bruxelles?' in Claeys, Paul-H. et al. (eds.) , *Lobbying, Pluralism, and European Integration,* Bruxelles, 1998, pp. 303-327.

Weidenfeld, Werner and Wessels, Wolfgang (eds.), *Jahrbuch der Europäischen Integration 1997/98,* Bonn, 1998.

Wiedmann, Thomas, 'Der Ausschuss der Regionen nach dem Vertrag von Amsterdam' in *Europarecht,* Heft 1, 1999, pp.49-86.

Information on Member States

Interviews conducted in the context of the research project

In the context of the preparation of this research project, the study team of the ECRF conducted several interviews with member of regional offices in Brussels in order to obtain information on the political practice of the policy making in the Member States as well as in the EU context. The information received in these interviews was used mainly as background information for the elaboration of the study. Further interviews were conducted by several country rapporteurs, who delivered preliminary reports for the research project.

Country Reports

The research team has asked several external experts to deliver country reports on the EU Member States, which served as important basis and source of information for the comparative analysis undertaken in this study. The research team would like to thank the country reports for their contribution. The following researchers contributed as external experts to the research project:

Boysen, Jens	College of Europe, Bruges, Belgium
Gustafsson, Hakan	Konsult / Eurofutures, Stockholm, Sweden
Hoetjes, Bernhard	Clingendael Institute, The Hague, The Netherlands
Lynch, Philip, Dr.	University of Leicester, UK
Lyubayeva, Alona	University of Leuven, Belgium
Mitsilegas, Valsamis	University of Leicester, UK
Pirc, Tatjana	College of Europe, Bruges, Belgium
Raffini, Daphnée	Université libre de Bruxelles, Belgium
Ritter, Michael	University of Salzburg, Austria
Ryynänen, Aimo, Prof. Dr.	University of Tampere, Tampere, Finland
Wharton, Barry, Dr.	Unviersity of Limerick, Ireland
Woelk, Jens, Dr.	European Academy Bolzano, Italy

Austria:

Dachs, Herbert (ed.), *Handbuch des politischen Systems Österreichs: Die zweite Republik*, Wien, 1997.

European Commission, Regional development studies, *The EU compendium of spatial planning systems and policies: Austria*, Luxembourg, 2000.

Falkner, Gerda and Müller, Wolfgang C. (eds.), *Österreich im europäischen Mehrebenensystem: Konsequenzen der EU-Mitgliedschaft für Politiknetzwerke und Entscheidungsprozesse*, Wien, 1998.

Schindegger, Friedrich, *Raum. Planung. Politik. Ein Handbuch zur Raumplanung in Österreich*, Wien, 1999.

Bodenhöfer, Hans Joachim, 'Bildungspolitik' in: Dachs, Herbert et al. (Hg.), *Handbuch der österreichischen Politik*, 3. Auflage, Wien: Manz Verlag, 1997, pp. 592-607.

Brenner, David, *Österreichs Arbeitsmarktpolitik. Ein Porträt unter Berücksichtigung des Wandels der Arbeitsmarktverwaltung*. Diplomarbeit, Salzburg, 1999.

Deußner, Reinhold et al., *Transeuropäische Netze und regionale Auswirkungen auf Österreich. Analyse des Ausbaus der hochrangigen Verkehrsinfrastruktur unter besonderer Berücksichtigung der Erreichbarkeit*, Schriftenreihe der Österreichischen Raumordnungskonferenz, Nr. 147, Wien, 1999.

Fallend, Franz, 'Kabinettsystem und Entscheidungsfindungsprozesse in den österreichischen Landesregierungen' in: Dachs, Herbert; Fallend, Franz and Wolfgruber, Elisabeth (Hg.), *Länderpolitik:Politische Strukturen und Entscheidungsprozesse in den österreichischen Bundesländer*,Wien.: Signum Verlag, 1997, pp. 231-354.

Fischer, Heinz, 'Das Parlament' in Dachs, Herbert et al. (Hg.), *Handbuch der österreichischen Politik*, 3 Auflage, Manz-Verlag, Wien, 1997, pp. 99-121.

Frey, Eric, 'Regionalismus in der EU' in Strejcek, Gerhard and Theil, Michael (Hg.), *Regionalisation in Österreich und Europa. Eine Untersuchung über rechtliche, politische und ökonomische Aspekte regionaler Entwicklungen*, WUV-Verlag; Wien, 1996, pp. 28-56.

Hackl, Elsa, *Das Österreichische Bildungssystem in Veränderung. Bericht an die OECD über die geplante Diversifikation des Bildungssektors*, Bundesministerium für Wissenschaft und Forschung, Wien, 1993.

Huber, Wolf, 'EU-Regionalpolitik und das Prinzip der Partnerschaften' in Staudigl, Fritz and Fischer, Renate (Hg.), *Die Teilnahme der Bundesländer am europäischen Integrationsprozess*, Schriftenreihe des Instituts für Föderalismusforschung, Band 66. Braumüller, Wien, 1996, pp. 97-104.

Kiefer, Andreas, *Die österreichische Delegation im Ausschuß der Regionen (AdR)*, Schriftenreihe des Landes-Europabüros, Nr. 3, Salzburg, 1996.

Kiefer, Andreas, 'Die österreichischen Länder und Gemeinden im Ausschuß der Regionen (AdR) der Europäischen Union unter Berücksichtigung der Koordinationsmechanismen in der österreichischen Delegation' in Staudigl, Fritz and Fischer, Renate (Hg.), *Die Teilnahme der Bundesländer am europäischen Integrationsprozess*, Schriftenreihe des Instituts für Föderalismusforschung, Band 66, Braumüller, Wien, 1996, pp. 30-60.

Kiefer, Andreas, 'Regionale Europapolitik aus Sicht der Landesverwaltungen' in Mayer, Stefan (Hg.), *Europa in den Ländern. Workshop zu Fragen der Europäischen Integration und Länderpolitik*, Dokumentationsband, Salzburg, 1998, pp. 32-36.

Lauber, Volkmar, 'Wirtschafts- und Finanzpolitik', in: Dachs, Herbert et al. (Hg.), *Handbuch der österreichischen Politik*, 3. Auflage, Manz-Verlag, Wien, 1997, pp. 545-556.

Lüschen, Gunther; Cockerham, William; van der Zee, Jouke et al. (Hg.), *Health Systems in the European Union. Diversity, Convergence and Integration*, 1995.

Luther, Karl Richard, 'Bund-Länder-Beziehungen: Formal- und Realverfassung' in Dachs, Herbert et al. (Hg.), *Handbuch der österreichischen Politik*, 3 Auflage, Manz-Verlag, Wien, 1997, pp. 907-919.

Morass, Michael, 'Die Praxis der Bund-Länder-Koordination in der EU-Politik' in Staudigl, Fritz and Fischer, Renate (Hg.), *Die Teilnahme der Bundesländer am europäischen Integrationsprozess*, Schriftenreihe des Instituts für Föderalismusforschung, Band 66, Braumüller, Wien, 1996, pp. 85-92.

Müller, Wolfgang C., 'Das Regierungssystem' in Dachs, Herbert et al. (Hg.), *Handbuch der österreichischen Politik*, 3 Auflage, Manz-Verlag, Wien, 1997, pp. 71-83.

Neisser, Heinrich, 'Die Verwaltung' in Dachs, Herbert et al. (Hg.), *Handbuch der österreichischen Politik*, 3 Auflage, Manz-Verlag, Wien, 1997, pp. 148-161.

Neuhofer, Hans, 'Gemeinden' in Dachs, Herbert et al. (Hg.), *Handbuch der österreichischen Politik*, 3.Auflage, Manz-Verlag, Wien, 1997, pp. 866-876.

Österreichische Raumordnungskonferenz, *Position Österreichs im Rahmen der Europäischen Raumentwicklungspolitik*, Schriftenreihe der Österreichischen Raumordnungskonferenz, Nr. 125, Wien, 1996.

Österreichische Raumordnungskonferenz, *Raumordnung in Österreich*, Schriftenreihe der Österreichischen Raumordnungskonferenz, Nr. 137, Wien, 1998.

Österreichische Raumordnungskonferenz, *Neunter Raumordnungsbericht*, Schriftenreihe der Österreichischen Raumordnungskonferenz, Wien, 1999.

Pelinka, Anton; Rosenberger, Sieglinde, *Österreichische Politik. Grundlagen, Strukturen, Trends*, WUV, Wien, 2000.

Schwarz, Wolfgang, 'EU-Regionalförderung in Niederösterreich – eine neue Qualität unserer Regionalpolitik', in: Schwarz, Wolfgang (Hg.), *Perspektiven der Raumforschung, Raumplanung und Regionalpolitik an der Schwelle zum 21. Jhdt. Beiträge aus Deutschland, Österreich und der Schweiz. Raumordnung, Landes- und Regionalentwicklung in Niederösterreich. Visionen – Konzepte – Realisierung*, Mitteilungen des Arbeitskreises für Regionalforschung, Vol. 26, 1996, pp. 226-241.

Schindegger, Friedrich, *Raum. Planung. Politik. Ein Handbuch zur Raumplanung in Österreich*, Böhlau, Wien, 1999.

Steger, Friedrich Michael, *Die Wiederentdeckung der Peripherie – Regionalismus und Regionalpolitik in Theorie und Praxis*, Dissertation, Salzburg, 1999.

Strejcek, Gerhard, 'Regionalisation in Österreich und Europa' in Strejcek, Gerhard and Theil, Michael (Hg.), *Regionalisation in Österreich und Europa. Eine Untersuchung über rechtliche, politische und ökonomische Aspekte regionaler Entwicklungen*, WUV-Verlag, Wien, 1996, pp. 3-27.

Strejcek, Gerhard, 'Die Reform der österreichischen Regionalpolitik im Lichte europarechtlicher Vorgaben und Ziele' in Strejcek, Gerhard and Theil, Michael (Hg.), *Regionalisation in Österreich und Europa. Eine Untersuchung über rechtliche, politische und ökonomische Aspekte regionaler Entwicklungen*, WUV-Verlag, Wien, pp. 86-125.

Tobanelli, Tanja Maria Magdalena, *Regionalförderung als Politikum. Die Teilnahme Österreichs an der EU-Strukturpolitik: eine Herausforderung für die Träger der Regionalpolitik. Die Förderungspraxis im Bundesland Salzburg*, Diplomarbeit, Salzburg, 1997.

Tondl, Gabriele, 'EU-Regionalpolitik in Österreich', in: Strejcek, Gerhard and Theil, Michael (Hg.), *Regionalisation in Österreich und Europa. Eine Untersuchung über rechtliche, politische und ökonomische Aspekte regionaler Entwicklungen*, WUV-Verlag, Wien, pp. 148-180.

Useful Internet Sources on Austria:

General information on Austria: http://www.oesterreich.com/

Ministry for Education, Science and Culture: http://www.bmuk.gv.at/

Salzburg: http://land.salzburg.at/

Steiermark: http://www.landeshauptmann.steiermark.at/

Information on the policy field of Education: http://www.vobs.at/Landesschulrat/

http://www.bmwf.gv.at/

http://www.austria.gv.at/

http://www.kulturpolitik.at/

http://www.bmaa.gv.at/

Federal government / Bundeskanzler: http://www.ris.bka.gv.at/

http://www.bmsg.gv.at/bmsg/

http://www.land-sbg.gv.at/

http://www.oerok.gv.at/

http://www.bmv.gv.at/

http://www.magwien.gv.at/

http://www.ams-sbg.or.at/

http://www.bmwa.gv.at/

http://www.stmk.gv.at/

Belgium:

Alen, André, *Der Föderalstaat Belgien : Nationalismus - Föderalismus - Demokratie* Mit dem Text der neuen Belgischen Verfassung, Schriftenreihe des Europäischen Zentrums für Föderalismus-Forschung, Band 4, Baden-Baden, 1995.

Alen, André, Handboek van het Belgisch Staatsrecht, Kluwer Rechtswetenschappen, Antwerpen, 1995.

De Grondwet van het Federale Belgie, Deurne, 1994.

European Commission, Regional development studies, *The EU compendium of spatial planning systems and policies: Belgium*, Luxemburg, 2000.

Fitzmaurice, John, *The Politics of Belgium. A Unique Federalism*, London, 1996.

Mörsdorf, Roland, *Das belgische Bundesstaatsmodell im Vergleich zum deutschen Bundesstaat des Grundgesetzes*, Lang, Frankfurt am Main, 1996.

Useful Internet Sources on Belgium:

Federal government: http://www.fgov.be/

Flemish Community: http://www.vlaanderen.be/

French-speaking Community: http://www.cfwb.be/

German-speaking Community: http://dglive.be/

Wallon Region: http://www.wallonie.org/

Province Antwerp: http://www.provant.be/

Denmark:

Christiansen, Thomas, 'Between 'In' and 'Out': EU Integration & Regional Policy-making', in: Lars Hedegaard and Bjarne Lindström (eds.), *The NEBI Yearbook 1999. North European and Baltic Sea Integration*, Springer, Berlin, 1999, pp. 193-208.

European Commission/EURYDICE/CEDEFOP, *Structures of the Education and Initial Training Systems in the European Union*, Office for Official Publications, Luxemburg, 1995.

European Commission, Regional development studies, *The EU compendium of spatial planning systems and policies: Denmark*, Luxemburg, 1999.

European Commission, DG Regio, *EC Structural Funds, Denmark – Single Programming Document 1994-96, Objective 3*, Office for Official Publications, Luxemburg, 1996.

European Commission, DG Regio, *The EU compendium of spatial planning systems and policies – Denmark (Regional Development Studies - 28 C)*, Office for Official Publications, Luxemburg, 1999.

EURYDICE, *Two decades of reform in higher education in Europe: 1980 onwards*, EURYDICE, Brussels, 2000.

Frissen, P.H.A., et al. (eds.), *European Public Administration and Informatization*, IOS Press, Amsterdam/Oxford/Washington/Tokyo, 1992.

International Energy Agency, *Energy Policies of IEA Countries. Denmark 1998 Review*, IEA, Paris, 1998.

Lyck, Lise, *Denmark and EC membership evaluated*, Pinter, London, 1993.

OECD, *Reviews of National Policies for Education. Denmark: Educating Youth*, OECD, Paris, 1995.

Wieslander, Anna, 'Building the Øresund Region' in Lars Hedegaard and Bjarne Lindström (eds.), *The NEBI Yearbook 1999. North European and Baltic Sea Integration*, Springer, Berlin, 1999, pp. 239-255.

Useful Internet Sources on Denmark:

Foreign Ministry: http://www.um.dk/

Ministry of Education: http://www.uvm.dk/

Danish Parliament: http://www.folketinget.dk/

Directory of websites of Danish government ministries and agencies: http://www.gksoft.com/govt/en/dk.html

Ministry of Health: http://www.sum.dk/health/

National Association of Local Governments in Denmark (NALAD): http://www.kl.dk/

Ministry of Culture: http://www.kulturministeriet.dk/

Ministry of Transport: http://www.trm.dk/

Ministry of Research: http://www.fsk.dk/

Ministry of Environment and Energy: http://www.mem.dk/

Danish Association of County Councils: http://www.arf.dk/

Danish agency for the promotion of educational exchange: http://www.icu.dk/engelsk/

Ministry of Labour: http://www.am.dk/

Kommunernes Landsforening: Local Government in Denmark, http://www.kl.dk/

Ministry of Foreign Affairs (Denmark): http://www.um.dk/

Ministry of Health (Denmark) (ed.) 1999, The Danish Health Care Sector, Kopenhagen, available at: http://www.sum.dk/publika/status

France:

AJDA , numéro spécial « Culture et service public », Ed. Le Moniteur, Paris, 2000.

'Les collectivités locales et initiative privée en matière de télécommunications', in *AJDA*, Ed. Le Moniteur, Paris, December 1999, p. 965.

Borgetto, Michel, *Droit de l'aide et de l'action sociale*, Montchrestien Domat, Paris, 3 ème édition, 2000.

Christadler, Marieluise and Uterwede, Henrik, *Länderbericht Frankreich. Geschichte, Politik, Wirtschaft, Gesellschaft*, Opladen, 1999.

Congrès des pouvoirs locaux et régionaux de l'Europe, *Rapport sur la démocratie locale et régionale en France*, Conseil de l'Europe, 2000.

Durand, Emmanuel, *Les collectivités territoriales en France*, Paris, 1994.

European Commission, Regional development studies, *The EU compendium of spatial planning systems and policies: France*, Luxemburg, 2000.

Hardy, Jacques, *Les collectivités locales*, Paris, 1998.

Moreau, Jacques and Truchet, Didier, *Droit de la santé publique*, Mémentos Dalloz, 3rd edition, 2000.

Moussis, Nicolas, *Guide des politiques de l'Europe*, Ed. Mols, Paris, 4th edition, 1999.

Gélabert, Marie-Christine, Rapport sur l'avenir de la décentralisation (sous l'angle des finances locales), to be published.

Rapport d'information du Sénat, N°157 *L'avenir des fonds structurels européens dans le cadre de l'agenda 2000*, 1997-1998.

Rémond, Bruno and Blanc, Jacques, *Les collectivités locales*, Presses de Sciences Po, Paris, 1992.

Rémond, Bruno, *La région: une unité politique d'avenir*, Montchrestien, Paris, 1995.

Pontier, Jean -Marie, Ricci, Jean-Claude and Bourdon, Jacques, *Droit de la culture*, 2nd edition, Dalloz, Paris, 1996.

Written Senate question No. 9879 of 30 July 1998.

Written Senate question No. 13866 of 4 February.

Written Senate question No. 25322 of 18 May 2000.

Written National Assembly question No. 17553.

Finland:

Committee for Urban Policy, *A Portrait of Finnish Cities, Towns and Functional Urban Regions*, The Finnish Urban Indicator System, Ministry of the Interior, Helsinki 1999.

European Commission, Regional development studies, *The EU compendium of spatial planning systems and policies: Finland*, Luxemburg, 1999.

Ministry of Education, *Education in Finland*, Vammala, 2000.

EUREGIO EGRENSIS and PÄIJÄT-HÄMEEN LIITTO, *A Trans-National Network. Report on the Previous Collaboration and the Prospects of Cooperation. EUREGIO EGRENSIS and Regional Council of Päijät-Häme*, Lahti, 1998.

Association of Finnish Local and Regional Authorities, *Finland's Regional Councils: Work to promote the prosperity of their regions*. Helsinki, 1998.

Finnish Association of Local Government Studies, *Finnish Local Government Approaching the New Millenium*, Finnish Local Government Studies, vol. 3/1999, English issue, Vammala, 1999.

Hautamäki, Antti, *Towards the Joint Responsibility of Local and Central Government. New Directions for Local and Central Government Relations*, Ministry of the Interior 3/1995, Helsinki, 1995.

Government of Finland, *High-Quality Services, Good Governance and a Responsible Civic Society, Guidelines of the Policy of Governance*, The Government Resolution 16.4.1998, Helsinki, 1998.

Government of Finland, *High-Quality Services, Good Governance and a Responsible Civic Society, Guidelines of the Policy of Governance*, Background Material, Helsinki, 1998.

Hult, Juhani and Erkki Mennola (eds.), *Regional Development of Our Own, Views from the New EU Member States*, University of Joensuu, 1997.

Kangas, Anita, 'Finnish Municipal Cultural Policy in Transition' in Oulasvirta, Lasse, *Finnish Local Government in Transition*, Finnish Local Government Studies 4/1995.

Korttila, Kirsi and Kukkanen, Leea, *Will the municipal primary health care differentiate?* Summary, The Association of Finnish Local and Regional Authorities, Helsinki, 1999.

Ministry of the Interior, *Selvitys kuntien itsehallinnollisesta asemasta. Kuntien itsehallintohankkeen raportti, Summary and estimate of the current status of municipal self-government,* 3/2000, Helsinki, 2000.

Modeen, Tore (ed.), *Public Administration in Finland,* Finnish Branch of the International Institute of Administrative Sciences & Ministry of Finance & Administrative Development Agency, Helsinki, 1994.

Naschold, Frieder, *The Modernization of the Public Sector in Europe, A Comparative Perspective on the Scandinavian Experience,* Ministry of Labour, Helsinki, 1995.

Pryy, Iikka and Paikallisvaltion, loppu *Abstract: The End of the Local State,* University of Joensuu, Joensuu, 1998.

Association of Finnish Local and Regional Authorities and Ministry of Finance: *Quality Strategy for Public Services, Productivity for the Future,* Helsinki, 1998.

Rainesalo, Pirkko and Kangas, Anita, *Competencies and practice in European local and regional cultural policy,* Congress of Local and Regional Authorities of Europe; Twin working groups on culture, education and the media 27.9.1999.

Ministry of the Environment, *Reform in the Land Use Planning System, The New Land Use and Building Act of Finland,* Helsinki, 1999.

Ministry of the Interior, *Regional State Administration in Finland,* Helsinki, 1997.

Selovuori, Jorma (ed.), *Power and Bureaucracy in Finland 1809 – 1998*, Edita and Prime Minister's Office, Helsinki, 1999.

Stenvall, Jari and Risto Harisalo, *Aluehallinto 2000 – uudistuksen arviointi. Uutta ideaa etsimässä, English Summary: Evaluating Regional Administration 2000 Reform, In Search of a new idea*, Tampere, 2000.

Suomen, Kuntalaki, *The Finnish Local Government Act*, The Finnish Local Authorities, Helsinki, 1996.

Association of Finnish Local and Regional Authorities, *The World of Finnish Local and Regional Authorities*, Iisalmi, 1998.

Vihervuori, Pekka, 'Public environmental Law in Finland' in Seerden, René and Heldeweg, Michel: *Comparative Environmental Law in Europe. An Introduction to Public environmental Law in the EU Member States*, Antwerpen, 1996.

Useful Internet Sources on Finland:

Association of Finnish Local and Regional Authorities: http://www.kuntaliitto.fi/

Finnish Government: http://www.vn.fi/

Finnish Parliament: http://www.eduskunta.fi/

Ministry of Education Finland: http://www.minedu.fin/

Ministry of the Interior: http://www.intermin.fi/

Regional Councils: http://www.reg.fi/West Finland Alliance: http://www.wfa.fi/

Germany:

Anzenbacher, Arno, 'Bildungsbegriff und Bildungspolitik', in: *Jahrbuch für christliche Sozialwissenschaften*, 40, 12-37, 1999.

Arnold, Rolf and Fritz Marz *Einführung in die Bildungspolitik: Grundlagen, Entwicklungen, Probleme*, Stuttgart, 1979.

Bandelow, Nils C., *Gesundheitspolitik: Der Staat in der Hand einzelner Interessengruppen*, Opladen, 1998.

Benz, Arthur, 'Rediscovering Regional Economic Policy: New Opportunities for the Länder in the 1999s', in: Jeffery, Charlie (ed.), *Recasting German Federalism. the Legacies of Unification*, London, 1999, pp 177-196.

Burmeister, Hans-Peter, *Kultur ohne Projekt? Kulturbegriff und Kulturpolitik in heutiger Zeit*, Rehburg-Loccum, 1998.

European Commission *Convergences and divergences in European education and training systems: A research project commissioned by the DG XXII*, Luxemburg, 1999.

European Commission, Regional development studies, *The EU compendium of spatial planning systems and policies: Germany*, Luxemburg, 1999.

Europäische Kommission, *Schlüsseldaten zum Bildungswesen in der Europäischen Union*, Luxemburg, 1997.

Europäische Union and Ausschuß der Regionen, *Interkulturelle Bildung in der Europäischen Union: Lokale, regionale und interregionale Aktionen, Nachahmenswerte Beispiele*, Luxemburg, 1999.

Führ, Christoph, *Bildungsgeschichte und Bildungspolitik: Aufsätze und Vorträge*, Köln, 1997.

Fritsch, Anke, *Europäische Bildungspolitik nach Maastricht – zwischen Kontinuität und neuen Dimensionen: Eine Untersuchung am Beispiel der Programme ERASMUS/SOKRATES und LEONARDO*, Frankfurt/M, 1998.

Höhne, Dieter, 'Bedingungen einer neuen Regionalpolitik – Auf dem Weg in den Europäischen Binnenmarkt', in: Bodo B. Gemper (Hrsg.), *Symbiose oder Konflikt? Föderalismus – Demokratie – Marktwirtschaft*, Hamburg 1989.

Hofecker, Franz Otto, Michael Söndermann and Andreas Wiesand (ed.), *Kulturfinanzierung im Föderalismus / Financing Arts in Federal States*, München, 1997.

Hrbek, Rudolf, 'The Effects of EU Integration on German Federalism' in Jeffery, Charlie (ed.), *Recasting German Federalism. the Legacies of Unification*, London, 1999, pp. 217-233.

Jeffery, Charlie (ed.), *Recasting German Federalism. The Legacies of Unification*, London, 1999.

Karl, Helmut, *Transeuropäische Netze: Die infrastrukturpolitischen Aufgaben der EU*, Bonner Schriften zur Integration Europas, Bonn, 1997.

Karpf, Ernst (Hrsg.), *Europäische Städte und ihre Jugendlichen: Jugendpolitik und Jugendarbeit im Vergleich*, Frankfurt/M, 1997.

Leonardy, Uwe, 'The Institutional Structures of German Federalism', in: Jeffery, Charlie (ed.), *Recasting German Federalism. the Legacies of Unification*, London, 1999, pp. 3-22.

Müller-Solger, Hermann, *Bildung und Europa: Die EU-Fördermaßnahmen*, Bonn, 1997.

Münch, Ursula, *Sozialpolitik und Föderalismus: Zur Dynamik der Aufgabenverteilung im sozialen Bundesstaat*, Opladen, 1997.

Riege, Fritz, *Gesundheitspolitik in Deutschland, Aktuelle Bilanz und Ausblick*, Berlin, 1993.

Riege, Fritz, *Kurzer Abriss der Gesundheitspolitik, Das Gesundheitswesen in der Bundesrepublik Deutschland*, Frankfurt/M, 1999.

Schultze, Claus J., *Die deutschen Kommunen in der Europäischen Union. Europa-Betroffenheit und Interessenwahrnehmung*, Schriftenreihe des Europäischen Zentrums für Föderalismus-Forschung, Band 12, Baden-Baden, 1997.

Suntum, Ulrich van, *Verkehrspolitik*, München, 1986.

Walther, Michael, *Verkehrspolitik in der Bundesrepublik Deutschland – Verselbständigung und Politische Steuerung –* Dissertation, Balingen, 1996.

Schröder, Meinhard, *Europäische Bildungspolitik und bundesstaatliche Ordnung*, Baden-Baden, 1990.

Weber, Kathrin, *Die Bildung im europäischen Gemeinschaftsrecht und die Kulturhoheit der deutschen Bundesländer*, Baden-Baden, 1993.

Wehling, Hans-Georg, *Bildungspolitik*, Stuttgart, 1997.

Wennemann, Martina, *Bildungspolitik und Bildungsentwicklung: Gesetzgebung und ihre Auswirkungen in der Jugend-, Erwachsenen- und Weiterbildung*, Opladen, 1999.

Winter, Klaus, *Die Entwicklung nationaler Bildungsungsysteme unter den Bedingungen der Europäischen Vereinigung*, Oldenburg, 1997.

Woischnick, Eckart, *Jugendpolitische Konzeption der Landesregierung*, Ministerium für Kultus und Sport Baden-Württemberg

Greece:

In Greek

Hlepas, N.-K., *Local Government in Greece. The Dialectic Antagonism of Decentralisation with Local Government*, Sakkoulas, Athens, 1999.

KEDKE, Special Conference: *Economic Independence for the Citizen, for Development, for Greece*, Halkidiki, 4-6 May 2000.

Makrydimitris, A. and N.-K. Hlepas, 'The Problematic of the Unification of OTA and the 'Ioannis Kapodistrias' Programme' in A. Makrydimitris, *Governance and Society. Public Administration in Greece*, Themelio, Athens, 1999.

Papandreou, V., Speech in KEDKE Annual Conference, September 2000.

Polyhronopoulos, P., 'Municipal Regional Theatres and Municipal Conservatoires' in EETAA, *Culture and Local Democracy*, Athens, 1994.

Venizelos, E., 'Constitutional Revision and Local Government' in Ta Nea newspaper, 26.10.2000.

To Vima newspaper, 'Multi-speed Cultural Network', 22.10.2000.

In English

Andrikopoulou, E., 'Whither Regional policy? Local Development and the State in Greece' in M. Dunford and G. Kafkalas (eds.), *Cities and Regions in the New Europe: the Global-Local Interplay and Spatial Development Strategies*, Belhaven Press, London, 1992.

Bullmann, U., 'The Politics of the Third Level' in *Regional and Federal Studies*, vol.6, no.2, 3-19, 1996.

Committee of the Regions, *Regional and Local Democracy in the European Union*, CoR-Studies E- 1/99, 1999.

European Commission, Regional development studies, *The EU compendium of spatial planning systems and policies: Greece,* Luxemburg, 2000.

Loughlin, J., 'Regional Autonomy and State Paradigm Shifts in Western Europe' in *Regional and Federal Studies*, vol. 10, no. 2, 10-34, 2000.

Ministry of Press and Mass Media, About Greece, Athens, 1999.

Papageorgiou, F. and S. Verney, 'Regional Planning and the Integrated Mediterranean Programmes in Greece' in *Regional Politics and Policy*, vol. 2, nos. 1 and 2, 139-161, 1992.

Paraskevopoulos, C.J., ' Social Capital, Institutional Learning and European Regional Policy: Evidence from Greece' in *Regional and Federal Studies*, vol. 8, no. 3, 31-64, 1998.

Paraskevopoulos, C.J., 'Social Capital and the Public-Private Divide in Greek Regions' in *West European Politics*, vol. 21, no. 2, 154-177, 1998.

Verney S. and F. Papageorgiou, 'Prefecture Councils in Greece: Decentralization in the European Community Context' in *Regional Politics and Policy*, vol. 2, nos. 1 and 2, 109-138, 1992.

Useful Internet Sources on Greece:

Ministry of Interior, Public Administration and Decentralisation: http://www.ypes.gr/

Ministry of Health and Social Care: http://www.ypyp.gr/

Ministry of Culture: http://www.culture.gr/

Ministry of Labour and Social Security- European Social Fund: http://www.forthnet.gr/labor-ministry

Organisation for Professional/Vocational Education and Training: http://www.oeek.gr/

General Secretariat of Youth: http://www.neagenia.gr/

Organisation of Employment of Human Resources: http://www.oaed.gr/

Ireland:

Coakley, John and Gallagher, Michael, *Politics in the Republic of Ireland*, Dublin, 1993.

European Commission, Regional development studies, *The EU compendium of spatial planning systems and policies: Ireland*, Luxemburg, 1999.

Neil, Cecily and Tykkyläinen, Markku (eds.), *Local economic development: a geographical comparison of rural community restructuring*, Tokyo, 1998.

Internet Sources on Ireland:

Government of Ireland: http://www.irlgov.ie/

Italy:

European Commission, Regional development studies, *The EU compendium of spatial planning systems and policies: Italy*, Luxemburg, 2000.

Große, Ernst Ulrich and Trautmann, Günter (eds.), *Italien verstehen*, Darmstadt, 1997.

Hine, David, *Governing Italy. The Politics of Bargained Pluralism*, Oxford, 1993.

Mühlbacher, Georg, *Italien auf dem Weg zu einem föderalen Staat?*, Occasional Paper no. 15, European Centre for Research on Federalism, Tübingen, 1999.

National Action Plan for Employment for 1999 (no date), available at: http://europa.eu.int/comm/dg05/emp&esf/naps99/naps_en.htm.

Seitz, Martina, *Italien zwischen Zentralismus und Föderalismus: Dezentralisierung und Nord-Süd-Konflikt*, Wiesbaden, 1997.

Useful Internet sources on Italy:

http://www.palazzochigi.it/

http://www.regioni.it

http://www.Regione.lombardia.it

http://www.regione.veneto.it

http://www.regione.toscana.it

http://www.regione.umbria.it

http://www.regione.calabria.it

http://www.costituzioniregionali.it

http://www.regione.vda.it

http://rap100.formez.it/programmi_2000-06.html

http://www.euroformazione.difesa.it

http://www.provincia.bz.it/ipe/infopoint_i.htm

http://www.univr.it/giuris/cde.htm

http://www.provincia.tn.it/Europa/cde/informazioni.htm

Luxembourg:

Useful Internet Sources on Luxembourg:

Policy documents: http://www.gouvernement.lu/gouv/fr/gouv/progg/index.html

Luxembourg government: http://www.gouvernement.lu/

Links to the ministries: http://www.etat.lu/

Netherlands:

Boeckhout, S., Hulsker, W. and Molle, W., 'The Netherlands' in Heinelt, H. and Smith, R. (eds.), *Policy networks and European structural funds*, Aldershot etc., Avebury, 1996, pp. 177-196.

Brom, S. and van der Wielen, H., 'Financial control and audit of EU-funds in the Netherlands' in *Public Management Forum*, Paris, Sigma-OECD, Nov.-Dec. 1999, pp. 10-11.

European Commission, Regional development studies, *The EU compendium of spatial planning systems and policies: The Netherlands*, Luxemburg, 1999.

Müller, Bernd (ed.), *Vorbild Niederlande? Tips und Informationen zu Alltagsleben, Politik und Wirtschaft*; Mit Niederlande-Lexikon, Münster, 1998.

Shetter, William Z., *The Netherlands in Perspective: The Dutch Way of Organizing a Society and its Setting*, Utrecht, 1997.

Useful Internet Sources on The Netherlands:

National Government: http://www.overheid.nl/

Portugal:

Briesemeister, Dietrich and Schönberger, Axel (eds.), *Portugal heute: Politik, Wirtschaft, Kultur*, Frankfurt am Main, 1997.

Decker, Alexander and Decker, Gudrun, *Portugal*, 2 ed. München, 1992.

Eichner de Lemos Lisboa, Sabine, *Portugal in der Europäischen Gemeinschaft: Chancen für ausländische Investoren*, Frankfurt/M, 1989.

European Commission, *The economic and financial situation in Portugal: Portugal in the transition to the EMU*, Luxemburg, 1997.

European Commission, Regional development studies, *The EU compendium of spatial planning systems and policies: Portugal*, Luxemburg, 2000.

Gallagher, Tom, 'Unconvinced by Europe of the Regions: The 1998 Regionalization Referendum in Portugal' in *South European Society & Politics*, 1/1999, pp. 132-148.

López Mira, Álvaro Xosé, 'Portugal: The Resistance to Change in the State Model' in *Regional & Federal Studies*, 2/1999, pp. 98-105.

Nataf, Daniel, *Democratization and Social Settlements: the Politics of Change in Contemporary Portugal*, Albany, 1995.

Tillmanns-Estorf, *Die Strukturpolitik der Europäischen Union: eine kritische Analyse ihrer Ziele, Instrumente und Maßnahmen am Beispiel Portugals*

Wiarda, Howard J., *Politics in Iberia: the political systems of Spain and Portugal*, 2 ed., New York, 1993.

Spain:

Barrios, Harrald, 'Negotiated decentralization in Spain. A framework for Centre-Periphery conflict accomodation', in Delmartino, Frank, Pongsapich, Amara and Hrbek, Rudolf (eds.): *Regional pluralism and good governance. Problems and solutions in ASEAN and EU-countries*, Baden-Baden, 1999.

CEDEFOP (European Centre for the Development of Vocational Training), *Vocational education and training in Spain*, Thessaloniki, 1996.

European Commission, Regional development studies, *The EU compendium of spatial planning systems and policies: Spain*, Luxemburg, 1999.

Genieys, William, 'Autonomous Communities and the State in Spain. The role of intermediairy elites', p. 167. In: Le Galès, Patrick and Lequesne, Christian (eds.), *Regions in Europe*, London and New York, 1997, p.167.

Guerra, Luis López, 'Spain: Regions and nationalities in Spain: the autonomous communities', in Färber, Gisela and Forsyth, Murray (eds.), *The regions - factors of integration or disintegration in Europe?*, Baden-Baden, 1996.

Hooghe, Liesbet, *Cohesion Policy and European Integration. Building Multi-level governance*, Oxford, OUP, 1996.

Keating, Michael, *The new Regionalism in Western Europe. Territorial restructuring and political change*, Cheltenham, Northampton, 1999.

Mateo, Juan Ferrer, 'Improving access to administration in Spain', in Batley, Richard and Stoker, Gerry (eds.): *Local government in Europe. Trends and developments*, London, 1991.

McGullion, Juan M.Arregui, *The role of the Spanish Autonomous Communities in the EU decision making process. The cases of Galicia and Catalonia*, Master Thesis, College of Europe, 1997.

Morana, Francesc, 'Mobilisations différentielles dans l'Espagne des Autonomies' in Négrier, Emmanuel and Jouve, Bernard (eds.), *Que gouvernent les régions d'Europe? Echanges politiques et mobilisations régionales*, Paris, 1988.

Morata, Francesc, 'La Catalogne et Barcelone dans l'Arène Politique de l'Union Européenne, in Balme, Richard (ed.), *Les politiques du Néo-Regionalisme en Europe*, Paris, 1996.

Newton, Michael T., *Institutions of Modern Spain. A Political and Economic Guide*, Cambridge 1997.

OECD, Working Papers, *The „School Workshop and Apprenticeship Centres" Programme and Development Promotion Units: A new tool for local development policy in Spain"*, Vol. IV, No. 60, Paris, 1996.

Querol Fernandez, Francisco, *Die Präsenz der spanischen Autonomen Gemeinschaften in Brüssel: das Büro der Regierung von Aragon in Brüssel*, in Peter Nitschke, *Die Europäische Union der Regionen, Subpolity and Politiken der Dritten Ebene*, Opladen, 1999, pp. 61-72.

Rovira, Enoch Albertí, 'El modelo español de participación de las Comunidades Autónomas en los asuntos europeos', in *Informe Comunidades Autónomas 1994*, Instituto de Derecho Público, Barcelona, vol. 1, 1995, pp.590-591.

Useful Internet sources on Spain:

Ministry of Education: http://www.mfom.es/

General Information on Spain: http://www.sispain.org/

Sweden:

European Commission, Regional development studies, *The EU compendium of spatial planning systems and policies: Sweden*, Luxemburg, 2000.

Jerneck, Magnus, Evaluation of Swedish Regional Experimental programme published in a report of Swedish inquiry commissions SOU64, 2000.

Gidlund, Janerik and Jerneck, Magnus, Local and Regional Governance in Europe, Evidence from Nordic Regions.

Government Bill 1998/1999:115, On their terms – A youth policy for democracy, justice and belief in the future.

Häggroth, S. and Peterson C-G, *Local Self Government in Transition in Sweden*, Swedish Ministry of Interior, 1998.

Häggroth, Sören et al, *Swedish local government: Traditions and reforms* Lidström Anders Local and Regional Democracy in Sweden, 1999.

Hjern, Benny, *Europeisk l'ancien régime EU och kommunerna*, 1999.

Jerneck, Magnus (eds), *Different Eurogames for Nordic countries, 1998.*

Johansson, Jörgen, 'Is there still a Swedish Model', in: Ingemar Elander et al, *Local self government. Housing and urban policy in Sweden and Russia, 1994.*

Larsson, Torbjörn et al., 'Government in Sweden: Structure, History' in Larsson, Torbjörn, *Recent Developments in the Surplus of the Intermediate Level in Europe.*

Lindholm, Evert, *The Nordic dimension*, paper presented at an IULA conference in Helsinki, 1998.

Stenelo, Lars-Göran and Jerneck, Magnus (eds), *The Bargaining Democracy in The Role of City Regions in Multi Level European Constitution*, 1996.

The National Board for Youth Affairs, *Review of national youth policy,* 1999.

The Swedish Association of Local Authorities, *Developments in the European Union and their effects on Sweden's local authorities* (Summary), 1995.

Useful Internet sources on Sweden:

Ministry of Health and Social Affairs: http://www.regeringen.se/

United Kingdom:

Elcock, Howard and Keating, Michael (eds.), *Remaking the Union. Devolution and British Politics in the 1990s*, Special Issue Regional and Federal Studies, 1/1998.

European Commission, Regional development studies, *The EU compendium of spatial planning systems and policies: United Kingdom*, Luxemburg, 2000.

Kingdom, John, *Government and Politics in Britain: An Introduction*, Cambridge, 1999.

Martin, Steve and Graham, Pearce, 'Differentiated Multi-Level Governance? The Response of British Sub-national Governments to European Integration' in *Regional and Federal Studies* Vol. 9, No. 2, 1999, pp. 32-52.

Mazey, Sonia and James Mitchell, 'Europe of the Regions: Territorial Interests and European Integration: The Scottish Experience' in Sonia Mazey and Jeremy Richardson (eds.): *Lobbying in the European Community*, Oxford, 1993, pp.95-121.

Useful Internet Sources on the UK:

UK Government Information (links to a large number of departments, executive agencies and public bodies): http://www.ukonline.gov.uk/

Department on Environment, Transport and Roads: http://www.detr.gov.uk/

Department of Education: http://www.dfee.gov.uk/

Department of Culture: http://www.culture.gov.uk/

Department of Health: http://doh.gov.uk/

Scottish Executive: http://www.scotland.gov.uk/

National Assembly for Wales. http://www.wales.gov.uk/index_e.html

Northern Ireland Executive: http://www.nics.gov.uk/

Information on Policy Fields

Borchardt, Klaus-Dieter, Teil XVII: 'Wirtschaftlicher und Sozialer Zusammenhalt' in Lenz, Carl Otto, *EG-Vertrag Kommentar*, Köln, 1999, pp. 1314-1341.

Coen, Marin, Kapitel 2: 'Der Europäische Sozialfonds' in Lenz, Carl Otto, *EG-Vertrag Kommentar*, Köln, 1999, pp. 1212-1223.

Council of the European Union, Council Regulation No 1260/1999 of 21 June 1999 laying down general provisions on the Structural Funds, Official Journal of the European Communities L 161/1, 1999.

Council of the European Union and European Parliament, Regulation No. 1262/1999 on the European Social Funds, 21.6.1999.

Council of the European Union and European Parliament, Regulation on the European Regional Development Fund, 1999.

Dieter, Rolf and Grüter, Josef Winfried, Teil XV: 'Transeuropäische Netze' in Lenz, Carl Otto, *EG-Vertrag Kommentar*, Köln, 1999, pp. 1280-1307.

Europäische Kommission, *Jugendpolitik in der Europäischen Union: Struktur und Ausbildung, Allgemeine und Berufliche Bildung Jugend*, Studien Nr. 7, Luxemburg, 1995.

Europäische Kommission, *Öffentliche Gesundheit in Europa*, Luxemburg, 1997.

Europäische Kommission, *Arbeitsprogramm der Generaldirektion für Regionalpolitik im Jahr 2000*,Brussels, 1999.

Europäische Kommission, *Strukturpolitische Maßnahmen 2000–2006, Kommentare und Verordnungen, Strukturfonds, Kohäsionsfonds, Strukturpolitisches Instrument zur Vorbereitung auf den Beitritt*, 1999.

Europäische Kommission, *EUREK – Europäisches Raumordnungskonzept, Auf dem Weg zu einer räumlich ausgewogenen und nachhaltigen Entwicklung der Europäischen Union*, adopted at the informal Council of Spatial Planning Ministers in Potsdam, May 1999, published by the Commission.

European Commission, *Report on Community Policies and Spatial Planning* (Working Document for the Commission Services), 1998.

European Commission, 'Regional Policy and Cohesion. Sixth Periodic Report on the Regions: Summary of Main Findings' in *Inforegio Fact Sheet*, 4 February 1999.

European Commission *Reform of the Structural Funds 2000-2006. Comparative Analysis*, June 1999.

Europäische Kommission, *Allgemeine und Berufliche Bildung, Jugend – eine Neue Programmgeneration (2000-2006), SOKRATES, LEONARDO DA VINCI, JUGEND, TEMPUS III*, 2000.

European Training Foundation, *Training and retraining in regions* (Report of the Advisory Forum. Subgroup final report), Torino, June 1999.

Fischer, Hans Georg, Kapitel 3. 'Allgemeine und berufliche Bildung und Jugend' in Lenz, Carl Otto, *EG-Vertrag Kommentar*, Köln, 1999, pp. 1222-1239.

Informal Council of Ministers responsible for Spatial Planning, *ESDP – European Spatial Planning Perspective. Towards Balanced and Sustainable Development of the Territory of the European Union* (Agreed at the Informal Council of Ministers responsible for Spatial Planning in Potsdam, May 1999).

Karl, Helmut, *Transeuropäische Netze: Die infrastrukturpolitischen Aufgaben der EU*, Bonn, 1997.

Klimke, Ulrich, 'Verkehrspolitik im zusammenwachsenden Europa' in *Zeitschrift für Verkehrswissenschaft*, 1995, pp. 66-76.

Knill, Christoph and Lenschow, Andrea, 'Neue Konzepte – alte Probleme? Die institutionellen Grenzen effektiver Implementation' in *Politische Vierteljahresschrift*, 4/1999, pp. 591-617.

Organisation for Economic Cooperation and Development (OECD), LEED Note Book No. 20: *Local Economies and Globalisation*, Paris, 1995.

Organisation for Economic Cooperation and Development (OECD), *Regional Competitiveness and Skills*, Paris, 1997.

Organisation for Economic Cooperation and Development (OECD), *Local Management. For More Effective Employment Policies*, Paris, 1998.

Organisation for Economic Cooperation and Development (OECD), *A Caring World. The New Social Policy Agenda*, Paris, 1999.

Prodi, Romano, *2000-2005: Shaping the New Europe* (Speech/00/41 of the President of the European Commission to the European Parliament), Strasbourg, 15 February 2000.

Prodi, Romano, *Reshaping Europe* (Speech/00/43 of the President of the European Commission to the Committee of the Regions), Brussels, 17 February 2000.

Useful Internet Sources:

http://www.europa.eu.int/ (Sections on the policy fields)

http://inforegio.cec.eu.int/

http://www.europa.eu.int/comm/education/youth.html

Committee of the Regions of the European Union

REGIONAL AND LOCAL POWERS IN EUROPE
Education and Youth, Culture, Public Health, Transeuropean Networks and Regional and Structural Policy

Luxembourg: Office for Official Publications of the European Communities

2002 — 301 pp. — 16 x 23 cm

ISBN 92-895-0151-0

Price (excluding VAT) in Luxembourg: EUR 35